FROM HERE TO THE STREETS

2012 Revised Edition

- **The Value of Integrity**

- **Goal Setting & Job Skills**

- **Tips for Interviewing**

- **Job Search Techniques**

- **Apprenticeship Programs**

- **Saving and Investing**

- **Complete Credit Repair Guide**

- **Setting & Maintaining a Budget**

- **Understanding Insurance**

- **Federal Bonding and Tax Credits**

- **Special Section on Small Business & Entrepreneurship**

- **Success Strategies for Ex-Offenders**

By: Joseph L. Chiappetta Jr.

Order this book online at www.trafford.com
or email orders@trafford.com

Most Trafford titles are also available at major online book retailers.

Printed in the United States of America.

ISBN: 978-1-4669-6767-0 (sc)
ISBN: 978-1-4669-6766-3 (e)

Trafford rev. 11/15/2012

 www.trafford.com

North America & international
toll-free: 1 888 232 4444 (USA & Canada)
phone: 250 383 6864 ♦ fax: 812 355 4082

ABOUT THE AUTHOR

Joseph L. Chiappetta was raised in Dauphin, Pennsylvania, near the state capitol, Harrisburg. He was an only child whose parents gave him an eclectic and diverse upbringing. By his ninth birthday, he was studying geology, astronomy, archaeology, and history in a special youth workshop at the William Penn Memorial Museum (now the Pennsylvania State Museum) under the direction of the curators and research staff. This continued for several years during which time he also studied judo, karate, and numerous outdoor sports and activities. At age 15, Joe had won his junior high school science awards and was participating in martial arts demonstrations throughout the Central Dauphin School District and all over central Pennsylvania. In his senior year, Joe was serving on the senior class council, doing a magic act in the yearly talent show, and working at Commonwealth National Bank as part of a student work program. He later took the Army entrance exam and scored the highest grade possible.

Following that part of his life, Joe took an interest in small business ownership and successfully opened and operated his own karate dojo, limousine service, computer sales company, and many other sales-based ventures. During these years, Joe's life took many turns in the wrong direction. Despite his many opportunities and skills, he turned to white collar crime and eventually ended up in and out of prison. During his current Arizona sentence he finally found a new calling: helping others. He started to work as a teacher's aide and helped his fellow inmates obtain high school equivalency diplomas. Since then, he has helped hundreds of students achieve this goal. A prison teacher saw Joe's potential and gave him an opportunity to assist her with an employability class. By early 2004, he had drafted an updated version of this course for his Unit Deputy Warden.

The experience has changed Joe's life as well. Redirecting his energy and talents towards helping others rather than taking from them has put his own life back on track after 20 years of personal failures. Joe is currently enrolled in three colleges studying business administration, emergency management, entrepreneurial development, and computer concepts. He is also continuing to develop his pre-release and employability course into a full range transitional program with the help of his teacher at Central Arizona College. He also studies under Professor Richard Shelton in a creative writing workshop. At his current facility, Joe is employed as an administrative clerk and substance abuse programs facilitator.

Special Thanks

After nine years of writing, teaching, and creating programs as an incarcerated inmate, I've learned that any success I may have achieved in this venue is a direct result of the amazing social network that I've been blessed with.

It all started with teachers like Dayleanne Wilson, Professor Richard Shelton, Sonia Vernon, Lisa Black, John Borquez, and Ms. Schmidt. The incredible wardens I've worked under have provided the necessary approvals. Without their support the programs could never have existed nor been utilized. Deputy Wardens like Ms. Simon, Mr. Curran, and Ms. Rider. In prison, security trumps everything. Security staff can torpedo a positive program as easily as the time it takes to voice, email, or telephone a single concern. In my experience, the majority of security officers were extremely helpful. Captain Iovino, Captain Higginson, Lt. Ping, Lt. Vance, and many others unlocked the doors and gave these programs a chance. Programs staff always worked side-by-side with me in these classes throughout their implementation and facilitation. Thanks to COIII Meitzer, COIII Holler, COIII Hook, COIII Felkins, COIII Grabowski, COIII Mayo, and even higher ranking staff like COIV Savinen and COIV Cottrell. Many sergeants and other uniformed staff have provided daily assistance. There are far too many to list. My amazing Licensed Substance Abuse Counselors, Colleen Fitzpatrick-Rogers and Jim Pitts, have fully supported my programs. Professor John Crosby and Professor Matt Wood of Central Arizona College provided guidance and support.

And then there are my teammates. As a wise coach once said, "There's no 'I' in the word TEAM. Other talented and proactive inmates have been my constant and daily support system in the trenches. My partner and adopted brother Troy Froehlich, and amazing friends like Dave Zorawski, Paul Sparks, Sam Roberts, Joshua Savage, John Zurawski, and Clifford Lacy. Super talented co-workers like Tommy Hunt, Gary Shepherd, Anthony Stearns, Andrew Cerny, Danny Almeida, Amidad Orduno, and many others.

Finally, my amazing family . . . My parents, married 50 years and always supporting, assisting, and often rescuing me from the many crazy situations I've encountered. My beautiful wife, Jeanne . . . the most loving and generous soul I've ever met.

Thank you all for making this possible.

Joseph L. Chiappetta Jr.
2012

About This Book

The corrections employee who inspired me to design this book knew what most of you reading this already know . . . that the only hope that more than 90% of incarcerated inmates nationwide have for not returning to prison is steady employment.

There are numerous books on this subject already and most of them say the same things. It's also fair to say that most are accurate. This course doesn't try to reinvent the wheel, so to speak, but instead gives a step-by-step guide for preparing and facilitating a Pre-Release Employability Class in a corrections environment. Prison inmates are, for the most part, challenged with a wide variety of social dysfunctions. Educational backgrounds vary as well. It is critical to make the Pre-Release Employability Class both user friendly and student specific for the challenges presented by the prison itself. Ultimately it's up to an individual whether or not he or she chooses to succeed or improve the quality of their life. The key is to make this goal in life attainable and realistic to the students, thus encouraging them to make that choice.

Remember that even the best plans in the world are nothing without good people to carry them out. If you're planning to teach or assist in a Corrections Pre-Release Employability Course, you must understand and believe in its benefits. Not only believe, but also participate by sharing your own personal experiences and opinions to the extent that policy allows. Only by interacting with the class on a more personal level will you get the respect and trust of your students. By operating in this capacity you become as important an asset to the course as the written material itself. The results of your efforts will be reflected in the future success stories from your students.

A Message For Corrections Administrators, Staff, and Inmates

If you are a Department of Corrections Supervisor, Administrator, Teacher, or an inmate doing self-study this type of book must look like quite a few others that you have seen or used. The major difference between this book and the rest is its origin. Its contents were created, facilitated, and developed by inmates under staff supervision, and successfully taught to over 1,000 inmates during a 9 year period in higher security corrections settings. Re-writing this course as an independent publication was the idea of the course's primary facilitator, who also wrote the material into an instruction manual for his unit deputy warden.

During the first 21 months that this course was taught, several former students that had been released wrote back to say that they had greatly benefited from this class. These previously incarcerated felons had found good paying jobs, decent housing, and a few had even repaired their credit and purchased houses using first time homeowner mortgage offers. In short, they used the information in this course and put their lives back on track. With that in mind, the author offers this material to you for use in your facility's programs. Please write the publisher a letter if you found this course or its materials useful. Thank you.

This is the revised 2012 version and is edited to meet copyright laws. Materials from sources are either open source, properly credited, or have written permissions. This new revision was completed in September 2012.

Send Letters to:

Joseph Chiappetta
P.O. Box 24-3664
Boynton Beach, FL 33424

Or Email to: joejr122@yahoo.com
Or Toll Free: 1-800-641-5964

From Here to the Streets
Course Syllabus

From Here to the Streets is an excellent self-study resource, but it is written as a manual for a course.

Who Should Teach/Facilitate This Course?

Anyone planning to teach or facilitate this course must have at least 3 (three) of the below listed:

Skills and Experience:
1. Professional Teaching Certificate or Degree
2. Previous Experience Teaching Similar Materials
3. Previous or Current Small Business Ownership
4. Successful Management Experience
5. Public Speaking Experience
6. Possess Steady Employment Experience

Teachers should choose inmate facilitators and teacher's aides who complement their own teaching style. The combined experience of the teacher and aides should include all of the above qualifications. Inmate Peer Mentors and Peer Educators are the best candidates.

Tips for Lessons

1. You are the teacher/facilitator. Rely on your own unique skills and experiences to make each lesson interesting and informative.

2. Rely on your student profile / initial assessments to determine the "tone" of each lesson. The introduction phase provides you with this information.

3. Keep things "flowing" . . . move from lecture to participation frequently throughout each lesson. Be sure to pause during the lecture to allow participation frequently throughout each lesson. Pause during the lecture to ask group questions that require *a show of hands*. This keeps the interest level high and makes the lesson more enjoyable. Positive energy within the group will remain higher if you do this.

4. use the lesson outline as a guide. Form your own version of each lesson that utilizes the materials provided plus any new or updated information that you bring in.

5. prepared. In a corrections setting the students are from a wide variety of backgrounds and are very intuitive. Make sure that you know all of the details of whatever you discuss and be prepared for pointed and intelligent questions.

6. Integrating materials. Every facility has its own pre-release and employability programs and materials. This book and its contents can be used to either supplement existing programs or provide an alternate approach. The cornerstone of this course is its flexibility. Providing useful information is the ultimate goal. From a variety of forms and exercises to the sample documents and study materials, any program will find something it can use or integrate into its lessons. Many other course books try to encourage replacement rather than collaboration. This material is designed to be used in any way the program facilitator chooses . . . dissected into parts or as a stand-alone program.

From Here to the Streets
Transition/Reentry Class

DO *YOU* HAVE WHAT YOU NEED TO RE-START YOUR LIFE?

DO YOU *KNOW WHAT IT TAKES TO GET A JOB?*
HAVE *YOU* EVER DONE A RESUME?
WHAT ABOUT AN INTERVIEW?

These are some of the questions that this class will be able to assist you with.

Learn How To:

- Write A Resume
- Conduct Yourself In An Interview
- Answer Tough Interview Questions
- Interview Practice / Actual Interview
- Fill Out Up-To-Date Applications
- Job Search Methods
- Set A Budget
- Understand Your Credit
- Understand Mortgages & Home Purchases
- Using The Federal Bonding Program

SIGN UP NOW!

- ✓ If you are interested in this class, please sign the Sign Up Sheet.
- ✓ Must be within 2.5 years of release date.
- ✓ Class is every Monday for approx. 3 months.
- ✓ Attendance is mandatory. Miss three classes and you'll be dropped.
- ✓ Limited space available / Serious Applicants Only!

LESSON 1

INTRODUCTION

Introduction

For those planning to teach this course, the introduction and screening process is critical. First impressions are lasting. Setting the mood and tone for the students is going to be a priority.

Begin by giving a brief explanation of the course. The best way to do this is to go through the "Course Syllabus" step-by-step, briefly explaining the various lessons. Be sure to keep the descriptions very basic. Don't allow a question and answer session. Let the students know that all of their questions will be addressed during and after the lessons themselves.

Using the "Survey Form" on a one at a time basis, personal introductions should be used to "break the ice." You can use a similar approach to those used by the 12-Step Program Group meetings. Have each student stand, state their name and give their own personal expectations of the class and themselves.

❖ "What do you want to get out of this class?" is the key question for each student. Here are some other questions that you should also consider asking your students:

❖ What kind of employment (if any) did you have before incarceration?

❖ What was the longest period of time that you worked for one place of employment and what was that profession?

❖ Are you certified in any field or know any special skills or training?

Keep the questions simple and inform your students to keep their answers simple too. There are three general types of answers that you will get from your students:

❖ Short, sloppy, and disorganized.

❖ Embellished and long-winded.

❖ Concise, short, and to the point.

The better of the three is concise, short, and to the point. Use the first two or three students for examples by "coaching" them through the questions and assisting them in forming their responses. You will see that the rest of the class will fall in line by example rather than lecture. Leading and teaching by example is the cornerstone of teaching anything in the correctional institution environment.

Use your class time wisely. This course is designed with three basic time lines in mind:

- ❖ 2 to 3 hours, one class per week.
- ❖ 45 minutes to 1 1/2 hours, two classes per week.
- ❖ One 8-hour "Fast Track".

This breakdown will take the 14 lessons to either a 14- or 7 week course. The 14-week course will have greater emphasis is on review, practice, and habit forming than the 7-week course that is more proactive and fast paced. As the teacher or facilitator, you must tailor your activities to best suit the students' needs and your teaching style. You must remember to give strict time limits so you don't end up running one lesson into another. Give at least one 15 minute break for every two hours of class. This should help to maximize your students' attention spans. The students that want to enroll into the "Fast Track" course should all be screened to include only highly motivated individuals who are too close to their release date which prevents them from participating in a regular course. Post a flyer and a sign-up sheet in the inmate housing area and other common areas for potential students. Then you'll be able to schedule an "Introduction Class" for those interested. The forms that are included can be used "as is." Customizing and adapting your lesson plans and materials to the unique nature of your inmates and institution will benefit the class many ways and you are encouraged to do so.

At the end of the Introduction, an assessment of each student should be made. The students themselves should be made aware of this fact before the process begins to encourage better performance. If your class space is limited you can use these results to determine which applicants may disrupt the class and to also try to sort multiple classes into more manageable groups. Make notes on each student's survey form during the interviews to identify and evaluate the student's performance. The maximum recommended number of students for this class is twenty (20). You will need at least one teacher/facilitator and one student aide. As the students begin to distinguish themselves, a few students from within the group may be chosen to assist in certain activities based upon their understanding of the materials and progress within the course. The physical location and choice of help will always be different depending upon the security level of your facility. The number of students and supervising personnel will also vary. This course gives only the structure, not the specifics. Flexibility is the key to success here.

Finish the Introduction with a brief overview of the lessons ahead. Remind the applicants that most of the work will be on their shoulders and only motivated individuals meeting the criteria will be chosen for the course. Try to keep that feeling of "qualification" alive in all future sessions to get the maximum performance out of the class.

Student Application

NAME: _____

DOC #: _____   HOUSING LOCATION: _____

How many years do you have left in prison?

_____

Why is it important that you get a job when you are released?

_____

_____

_____

What would you like to learn from this class?

_____

_____

_____

If you were selected for this class what would be some of your goals?

_____

_____

_____

How serious are you about committing (2) hours per week to this class? (Circle one)

NOT AT ALL   SOMEWHAT   EXTREMELY

---

3 unexcused absences and you will be dropped from the class

Student Interview
Evaluation Form

Student Name and I/M #: _____

Posture:

Eye Contact:

Verbal Skills:

Overall Score (1-10):

Comments:

Recommend for Class (yes/no):

Fast Track Class (yes/no):

Facilitator/Aide:

Opening Speech to Class

The transition to life after prison is a difficult process. This course is designed to help you bridge the gap from here to there. If you pay attention, take notes, and are serious about this class, you will be successful.

This course has many lessons and a lot of information to absorb. Taking notes and asking questions is the only way you will get the maximum benefit from the material. Your Student Folders contain a lot of what you will need, but paper and a pen or pencil is required. Your notes will be reviewed and shared with the class periodically, so do your best to pay attention and ask for things to be repeated if necessary. Please be polite and raise your hands for questions, also try to keep your questions short and to the point. The final lesson is actually a Question and Answer session, so remember to keep track of anything you feel you need more information about.

Let's get started . . . .

Tips for a Successful Class

- Clearly state the ground rules for the class, and enforce them.
- Always give clear directions and encourage questions.
- Require all students to bring their folders and pens or pencils. This class is about preparing for real world situations. Requiring the students to come prepared is a priority.
- Focus on lecture rather than text. Only use the written materials as a guideline.
- Require students to take notes, and periodically review those notes.
- Be prepared to update or add information at any time during the course. Facts and figures change daily, as do addresses and telephone numbers.
- Be flexible. The lesson plans are based on the outline, but are not rigid. Every class is different, so be prepared to alter or rearrange the lessons to suite your classes' specific needs.

LESSON 2

GOALS

Reminder:

Each lesson section contains helpful materials, but the way they are presented is up to the teachers and facilitators. Most of the core concepts are common sense and second nature to those selected to teach this course; so the key is in sharing that experience with the students.

Setting Goals

Getting anyone to sit down and set realistic goals is a challenge. For the most part the majority of people in general have no clear idea how to organize their thoughts or set up an effective Plan of Action. Teaching this concept to inmates is even more problematic. To get good results out of this lesson, a form is provided to use. The instructions are simple . . . start the students with long-term goals and work those into short-term goals.

Basically, the teacher should follow the pre-printed materials provided and focus on getting the students to put what starts as abstract ideas into clear and more organized statements. Also use the following examples for short-term and long-term goals:

Sample—Short-Term Goals (1 to 4 weeks)

> 1. **Show up to class prepared and on time**
> 2. **Stay out of trouble**
> 3. **Keep up with my exercise**
> 4. **Catch up on my reading or letter writing**

Short-Term Goals are everyday things that often get ignored. This lack of discipline is an important point to discuss with the class, because the "little things" always seem to be easier to put off or forget. When building a house, the foundation has to be strong. Staying current with short-term goals is very much like building a foundation for one's life. How can anyone hope to make plans for 6 months to a year down the road when they can't organize a few weeks? The answer is—they can't. Teaching the students to recognize this simple truth is important. Anyone can dream of wonderful possibilities for the next few years. There's plenty of time; so there's no rush, right? Wrong.

Sample—Long-Term Goals

> 1. **Getting out of prison with a plan**
> 2. **Staying out of prison**
> 3. **Getting a job**
> 4. **Continuing my education**
> 5. **Buying a home**
> 6. **Raising my children**
> 7. **Fixing my marriage or relationship**

"Working toward Long-Term Goals is like finishing a jigsaw puzzle; the pieces are part of the overall picture, but by themselves . . . not clear at all."

Goal Setting Exercise #1

PICK AN ACHIEVEMENT OR GOAL THAT IS IMPORTANT TO YOU AND WRITE IT HERE:

_____

_____

Give details about this goal and what you would like to accomplish.

_____

_____

_____

Within the next two years, what three things could you do to move closer to this Goal?

1. _____

2. _____

3. _____

List at least three things you could do in the next thirty days to begin working towards this goal.

1. _____

2. _____

3. _____

LESSON 3

SKILLS

Tips for Lesson

- ❖ Make copies of the "Skills Exercises" and have the students complete them. (Time: 10 minutes.)

- ❖ Review the results by going around the class, student by student, and discussing the various skills chosen. (Time: 20 to 30 minutes.)

- ❖ Ask students if they have ever wanted to use their skills top open and operate their own business. Be sure to have each student read their skill selections from the completed Skills Exercise Sheet. Challenge those who failed to select at least (10) ten skills from the various categories and explain how everybody has a certain amount of skills from everyday life. Be sure to use your own knowledge and experiences in this and all other lessons. (Time: 30 minutes to 1 hour).

KNOWING YOUR SKILLS

1. Personal-Management Skills

- ❖ Punctual
- ❖ Honest
- ❖ Reliable
- ❖ Patient
- ❖ Follow Instructions
- ❖ Self-motivated

2. Transferable Skills

- ❖ Speaking in Public or Groups
- ❖ Planning and Organizing
- ❖ Supervising Others
- ❖ Increasing Sales
- ❖ Problem Solving
- ❖ Instructing Others

3. Job-Related/Result of "On-the-Job Training"

- ❖ Specialty Equipment Skills
- ❖ Computer-related Skills
- ❖ Medical-related Skills
- ❖ Operating Heavy Equipment

Job Skills Exercise #1
Examine Your Skills

Based on your work, volunteer, military, educational experience, and/or total life experience. Make a list of the skills that you possess. Next, circle skills and character traits that you believe are your strongest. Now list those words on a separate piece of paper and write an example to show that you possess those skills. These will be your transferable skills that you will want to feature on your application, resume, and in the interview responses.

Leadership	**Personal Interaction**	**Dealing with data and I.T.**
Competitive	Aided	Analyze data
Decisive	Administer	Audit records
Delegate	Answered questions	Budgeting
Direct others	Attended/assisted others	Calculate/compute
Explain things to others	Counsel others	Compile
Initiate new tasks	Demonstrate	Detail oriented
Make decisions	Instruct	Document research
Mediate problems	Listen	Evaluate
Motivate people	Negotiate	Investigate
Negotiate agreements	Patient	Keep financial records
Planning	Supervise	Locate information
Result-oriented	Tactful	Manage money
Take risks	Teaching	Posted
Conduct meetings	Tolerant	Programmed
Self-confident	Trusting	Proofread
Solve problems	Tutored	Record facts
Generate ideas	Understanding	Take inventory
Artistic/Creative	**Key skills**	**Using language**
Artistic	Coordinated tasks	Articulate well
Drawing	Instructing others	Communicate verbally
Expressive	Implement	Correspond with others
Perform, act	Managing resources	Create new ideas
Present artistic ideas	Managing people	Design
	Meeting deadlines	Develop/create
Dexterity	Serving the public	Encouraged
Assemble things	Negotiating	Greeted
Build things	Organizing projects	Justified
Construct/repair buildings	Performed	Presented
Drive, operate vehicles	Processed	Promoted
Fabricated	Provided	Published
Loaded	Scheduled	Speak publicly
Operating tools, machines	Served	Teamwork
Repair things	Supervised	Telephoned
Typed	Transported	Write clearly

Job Skills Exercise #2

Using the examples on the previous page as a guideline, choose five (5) job skills that you have and give an example of how you have used this skill.

Job Skill #1: _____

An example of how I have used this skill is:

_____

Job Skill #2: _____

An example of how I have used this skill is:

_____

Job Skill #3: _____

An example of how I have used this skill is:

_____

Job Skill #4: _____

An example of how I have used this skill is:

_____

Job Skill #5: _____

An example of how I have used this skill is:

_____

What job position do you feel would be perfect for your job skills? _____

LESSON 4

JOB RESEARCH

Tips for Lesson:

❖ Discuss "cold calling." Use forms for exercises.

❖ Use the "job research tools" page and discuss where, who, and how to look for employment.

❖ Review the basic concepts of Job Hunting and review the materials by allowing students to read and discuss each section.

NOTE: This lesson should be an overview of the basics. Only devote about 30 minutes to this lesson, but make the lesson interactive by going through each student's own previous experiences and your own.

Careers for Felons
From Buzzle.com

In these times of economic recession, it is difficult to find employment for the general population and even more so for convicts. There are limited industries that offer jobs to convicts, mostly at the entry-level. The government has introduced tax reforms and awards programs to encourage industries to hire felons. One of the acts is the Work Opportunity Tax Credit (WOTC), which offers businesses tax credit if they hire felons. Another initiative is the Workforce Investment Act, which offers training programs that help individuals find gainful employment. There is the Federal Bonding Program (FBP), run by the US Department of Labor, which guarantees job honesty of ex-felons for the first six months. The employer is provided, free of cost, a fidelity bond guarantee for employing a felon. This means the government takes guarantee of any loss to the company because of the felon.

The life of a felon is full of hardships. A stable job can provide some relief, but it's not easy to find one. On completion of their term, some convicts do realize their mistake and opt for a straight path, but this 'straight path' is full of hardships. Not revealing a conviction is not a wise option, as most firms opt for a background check before hiring. Networking is the key. To increase your chances of getting a good job, try contacting family, friends, pastor, etc., as referrals can help you build trust with the employer.

It is true that some criminal acts authorize the revocation or suspension of rights to employment in certain situations. Several states have laws pertaining to employment for felons. While these laws center on the fact that an individual cannot be denied employment merely because of prior conviction, they do come with added stipulations, like taking into account the severity of the offense or the time lapsed after conviction. In states like New York, Hawaii, and Minnesota, public employment agencies cannot deny a felon employment unless the crime committed and the job applied for are related directly or indirectly to each other. Furthermore, if the employer feels that the person is not suitable for the job because of his record, it is mandatory for him to give in writing his reasons. In most state, law enforcement agencies, corrections agencies, and jobs requiring the felon to be in contact with vulnerable population are excluded from these laws.

Although it might sound difficult to find industries that offer jobs to felons, there are opportunities in different sectors for someone with a criminal past. Anyone who is willing to rehabilitate and find gainful employment should understand that although the task is difficult, it is not impossible to find a job. Work opportunities for felons may be limited, but if you are willing to put in some hard work there are some industries which offer favorable opportunities.

Temporary Jobs

A convict under a supervised release program has to follow the regulations issued by his parole officer. In such circumstances, it may be ideal to search for agencies that provide temporary jobs for felons and pay on a daily or weekly basis. While truck driver is perhaps the best example of a temporary job for an ex-felon, other examples include laborer, courier, or other manual labor jobs. On the completion of his stipulated probation or parole period, the felon can start looking for permanent work that will offer better pay and better security.

Companies that Hire Felons

Big companies may find it difficult to hire felons, but many relatively smaller firms look for people who are work-oriented, especially firms where there is a lot of manual work to be done. Such places don't mind hiring felons after completing some basic formalities, such as mandatory drug testing. Driving, industrial work, construction, etc. are some areas that hire convicts. Several transport companies hire convicts as drivers, where the work ranges from long-distance transportation to neighborhood delivery.

Learning a particular trade, like masonry or cooking, can also be helpful, as the person can start his own small-scale business. Even some government agencies and church-based organizations can be felon-friendly employers. The Salvation Army's Prisoner Rehabilitation Program center has been encouraging ex-felons to participate in work release programs for many years. Lately, even the defense industry has begun hiring felons, depending on background and type of crime committed.

Armed Forces

One of the best avenues for jobs for ex-felons is the US Army. These jobs will not only give you a steady income, but will also give you respectability, and much-needed stability. The army runs a 'moral waiver' program under which it gives employment to people with a criminal background in different sectors like construction, maintenance, drivers, and clerks.

Nonprofit Organizations

Get on the Internet and find nonprofit organizations near you. Due to the nature of their work they have a more lenient attitude towards offering jobs to felons. If you don't get a job up front, start volunteering at a nonprofit organization (NPO) and get that experience on your resume. Then you can approach another NPO for paid employment.

Restaurant Jobs

This is one of the places that hire felons and has enough job opportunities if you are willing to start at an entry level. The restaurant industry has something known as the floating staff, meaning employees join and then they leave. This makes it simpler to get a job in this industry, as they are always on the lookout for a fresh pair of hands and legs.

Retail Services

Many jobs are available in the retail sector. The best options can be found with retail shops which are individually owned and are located in posh areas. The owners may be skeptical because of your record, but it is up to you to convince them how you've changed and want the chance to get your life back on track.

Online Jobs

If you have basic knowledge of computers, one of the avenues for jobs is the Internet. You could do online content writing, market research, data entry, surveys, etc. Telemarketing is another option to explore. Although some of these opportunities might be temporary, they offer the chance to make a decent wage. Agencies offer these jobs to felons, as they do not require interaction with clients or handling of office property.

Construction Jobs

Companies in this field are on the constant lookout for people willing to put in hard work. Many felons are hesitant to take these jobs as they don't want the laborer tag to get stuck on them. What they may not realize is that they can slowly advance in this field to become supervisors. Due to a low educational level of most felons, they generally start at the bottom and work their way up. Doing a good job can build your credentials and help when you apply for educational grants, which will help you further your education and your rise in the company. People with skills such as painting, plumbing, and machine operators have a good scope of employment in this sector.

Security Guard Jobs

You don't need a degree or a high school education for this. You can get a job with an agency that provides security to celebrities, houses, buildings, and offices. Remember, a background check will be done, and you will be asked questions about your crimes.

Others

Other industries that offer employment for convicts are Christian missionaries and the Salvation Army. Keep a look out for 'Help Wanted' signs around your neighborhood, and don't be embarrassed to approach these business owners. Seek advice and help from NPOs. Get in touch with the state employment office and enroll in their programs.

Use all of your contacts. Remember not to get picky about the jobs being offered. At this point, the most important this is getting that first job and beginning to get your life back on track.

Job Research

Most of you reading this have looked for a job before. Below is a checklist of the most common and effective resources for both job hunting and getting on your feet after being released from custody. If you are homeless, on a low income, or without family support, the following resources will help.

Job Research Tools

- ❖ Internet
- ❖ Yellow Pages
- ❖ One Stop Career Centers
- ❖ Federal Bonding Program
- ❖ Networking (Friends & Family)
- ❖ Old Jobs (co-workers and supervisors)
- ❖ Public Library
- ❖ Employment Agencies
- ❖ Help Wanted Notices
- ❖ Newspaper Classified Ads
- ❖ Word of Mouth
- ❖ Government Un-Employment Offices (Local, State, Federal)

Post-Release Resources

- ❖ Salvation Army/Goodwill
- ❖ Churches and Church Groups
- ❖ Halfway Houses/Shelters
- ❖ Food Banks

One Stop Career Centers

They are one of the best resources available to anybody looking for a job! Here are some of the free services that they provide:

- ❖ They give referrals for jobs based upon the applicant's skills and experience.
- ❖ They help set up interviews.
- ❖ They do resume writing for those who need help or do not have a computer.
- ❖ They provide useful tips, information, and up-to-date job market overview and analysis.

These are some things you can do at a One Stop Center:

- ❖ Set up a surety bond for employment. (See Federal Bonding Package)
- ❖ Look for a better job while working at your present employment.
- ❖ Surf the Internet, check your email, use fax machines, or work with a counselor.
- ❖ Pick up information and funding options for vocational training or college.
- ❖ Get transportation vouchers.
- ❖ Get clothing vouchers.
- ❖ Get food bank locations.
- ❖ Obtain information on where to look for health care insurance.

America's Service Locator
www.servicelocator.org

America's Service Locator (ASL) connects you to local offices where you can find employment, training, and other important resources.

NOTE: One Stop Career Centers are in most of the 50 states by one name or another. Call 1-877-US-2JOBS to locate and identify them.

Tips for Successful Cold Calling

❖ Use names as references whenever possible.

❖ Time your calls. Your best chances of getting through directly to a decision-maker are early in the morning and shortly before noon.

❖ Before you make your first cold call, write down the objective of that call. Write down key points you want to make during the conversation.

❖ Begin your conversation with a specific benefit for the employer. Sell yourself as an asset for the business you call.

❖ Dress for an interview while cold calling. Research has proven that those who are well dressed are also the most effective on the phone.

❖ Take these calls seriously. You never get a second chance to make a first impression.

Job Hunting 101

❖ Planning, research, and organization are necessary elements of any job search. Here are several important steps:

❖ Schedule your efforts. Know when and where you are going to look for work.

❖ Prepare for interviews. Select outfits fit for an interview. Ask a family member or a friend to help you practice answering questions.

❖ Spread the word. The more people who know you are looking for work, the better your chances of finding a job.

❖ Use different resources. Check want ads: call and visit employers for whom you would like to work: join networking groups.

❖ Use the Internet. If you do not have a computer at home, visit One Stop Centers or the public library. Be sure to check www.de.state.az.us and click on Job Fairs.

❖ Sell yourself. Make a list of your skills, emphasize how adaptable and flexible you are. Include hobbies and outside interests and activities.

❖ Be persistent. Ask interviewers if you can call them back at a specific time and date.

❖ Compile references. Have a list ready.

One Stop Centers list these types of jobs and many others. Here are sample listings:

❖ Custom Countertop Cabinetmaker. At least 2-3 years of experience performing custom countertop work with plastic laminates. Must have experience with routers, files and other equipment related to the job. $15-$20 per hour. Job Order AZ9171863.

❖ Welder/Fabricator. Requires welding certification and 2 years Mig & Tig welding and fabrication. Mechanically inclined. Steel-toed boots, glasses and back brace are musts. Job site: west Phoenix. $15 per hour. Job Order AZ9171267.

Improve Your Job Search

You've been searching for a new job, but just can't seem to find the right fit. Maybe it's time to throw out your own approach and try something different. Here are some strategies to get you started:

❖ **Set Realistic Expectations**

Setting realistic career expectations is key to conducting a successful job search. If you are not seasoned in your field of choice, look for positions that will let you broaden your skills. You may not secure that management job this time, but you will be well-positioned for future opportunities.

❖ **Review Your Resume**

Your resume may not be attracting the right attention, and it may be time to spiff it up a bit. Ask two or three people, preferably those with business or career experience, to critique your resume, and be open to their suggestions.

❖ **Reevaluate Your Approach**

Looking for a job full time is a job in itself. If you are only dedicating a few hours a week to your job search, consider stepping up your efforts. Expand the places you're looking and the time you're spending looking, contacting, and submitting applications.

❖ **Take a Break**

It may sound simple, but sometimes what you really need is to get away for the stress of job searching. If you can afford to, give yourself permission to take a week or two off. You will be surprised at how your outlook will change.

Sometimes all it takes is a little adjustment for things to click. Be open to making some changes in your job search strategy, and before you know it, you will be the one dispensing job search advice!

Job Research Exercise

Directions: Choose a job and try to research as many aspects of it as you can. Use any and all material at your disposal, including class discussion materials.

Job Title: _____

List the skills you need to have to do the job:

_____

Nature of the work:

_____

Working Conditions:

_____

Training, Other Qualifications, and Achievements:

_____

Job Description:

_____

Wages / Benefits:

_____

Related Occupations:

_____

Why did you pick this job?

_____

Apprenticeship Programs

What Is Apprenticeship?

An apprenticeship is a way people learn the skills they will need in the trade of their choice. These skills are learned through a planned program combining both training in the classroom and on the job supervision of a certified journeyman who has already mastered the trade.

The Classes

The classroom instruction is referred to as related training. This training takes approximately five hours a week and though classroom based, may also involve some home study. Classes are taught by craft workers and other skilled persons and are used to familiarize the apprentice with trade manuals and other educational and technical materials. Classes might be scheduled either during the day or the evening and each focus on an important area of background training. Examples of technical courses might be subjects like drafting, blueprint reading, mathematics or others. In many cases this instruction is given at an apprenticeship-training site of the craft involved, although other sites are also used. In many cases, training is also offered in a local community college, so students earn college credits while they study their trade.

The "On-The-Job Training"

On-the-job of training is an applied part of apprenticeship programs. It is here you work with and learn from experienced journeymen who are able to pass along their knowledge gained over years of actually doing the job. While you are training on-the-job, you receive wages for your work. One of the significant advantages of apprenticeship training is YOU EARN WHILE YOU LEARN. When you begin your apprenticeship, the starting wage is generally about 35%-50% of the journeyman wages. This rate increases about every six months as you satisfactorily work in the program. Near the end of training, an apprentice is a skilled craft worker and is earning about 95% of the journeyman wage. As you continue in your trade, your rate of pay increases with your knowledge and abilities.

Getting Started

Specific requirements vary among programs. There are generally four factors to consider: age, education, aptitude, and physical conditions. Based upon child labor laws, the minimum legal age for apprenticeship is 16. Most programs set the minimum age at 18, and some programs may require you to have a driver's license.

Education

Most programs require applicants to have a high school diploma or GED. Regardless of the level of education required, apprentices should have solid skills in reading, writing, and mathematics—all of which are essential in any of the skilled trades. Some programs also require applicants to have certain aptitudes demonstrated by passing specially designed tests, such as the GATB. These tests may measure abilities such as your dexterity, coordination or some other skill. Also most programs require good general health and stamina at a level that would make you physically fit for the requirements of the type of job you would perform. Assuming that you meet the basic requirements set by the apprenticeship program of your choice, the next step is formal application for the program. Once in the program, you will have several years of solid on-the-job and classroom training that will form the foundation for a career in the trade you have chosen. At the end of your apprenticeship training, you will receive a nationally recognized certificate stating that you are a fully qualified journeyman.

Certification as a Skilled Journeyman

Recognition as a skilled journeyman will increase your opportunities for good jobs and good pay nationwide. Your skills will set you apart from other workers and identify you as an individual who is better trained, more productive, and a safer worker.

Various Apprenticeship Trades

Asbestos Workers	Mining Industry Trades
Boilermakers	Operating Engineers
Bricklayers/Tile Setters	Outside Lineman
Building Maintenance Trades	Painters/Drywall Tapers
Carpenters/Cabinetmakers	Plumbers/Pipe Fitters
Drywall/Lathers/Millwrights	Printing/Graphic Arts Industry
Cooks and Chefs	Refrigeration Mechanics HVAC
Electricians	Roofing Industry Trades
Glaziers	Sheet Metal Trades
Iron Workers	Sprinkler Fitters
Machinist Trades	Teamsters—Drivers/Mechanics
Manufactures Industry Crafts	Tool and Die Makers
Mechanic Auto—Heavy Equipment	

Apprenticeship Programs

Information about apprenticeship programs can be obtained from One-Stop employment offices listed in the blue pages of your local telephone book. Apprenticeship information can also be obtained from union locals listed in the white pages of the telephone book or the Internet.

How to Apply to an Apprenticeship Program

❖ **CALL** and ask when applications are accepted. Some program take applications any time their office is open, others are only available a few hours a year. Make sure you don't miss an opportunity—get this information first!

❖ **FIND OUT** what documents you need to bring with you. The programs are required by the federal government to keep copies of certain documents. They will return your originals to you. They will NOT allow you to apply without all required documentation.

❖ **ASK** if they can send you any materials about their program. Most have printed materials or a brochure that will answer many of the questions you have. If, after reading those materials, you still have questions, then call the program office and ask for clarification. Ask if they have a website, if you have access to the Internet. Many programs provide excellent information on line.

❖ **DRESS** appropriately when you go in for the interview. For most apprenticeships, the rules are changed. Don't wear 'office' attire. Your best bet is a pair of pants and a shirt with a collar. You want to look neat and clean. Shoes should have a low heel. If you are female, keep your jewelry, hair, and makeup low-key. This is not a time to make a personal statement with your clothing or hair.

❖ Make sure you **TAKE A PEN** (one that you know writes!), a sharp pencil, and a list of addresses and phone numbers (from past employers or references) you may need in order to fill out your application. Be sure that you have the proper documents that the program requires. This may include such items as a birth certificate or driver's license. *Ask your references in advance for permission to use their names.*

❖ In your interview, **EMPHASIZE** your jobs and hobbies that indicate an interest in the outdoors, fixing or working on your home on your own or 'helping' with alterations or repairs. Also mention anything that indicates knowledge of what it is like to spend the day outside and a willingness to do so. If you like to garden, that's a good hobby to mention. If you like to crochet, don't mention it.

❖ **DON'T** take your children with you. They will get bored and cause problems both during the interview and the selection process. This may not be fair, but it's the way it is. Look at this as your first test of how well your child care system works.

LESSON 5

**PERSONAL
INFORMATION
CARDS**

What is a PIC Card?

A PIC Card is a 2"x3" card you can use in job hunting. It is similar to a business calling card. Cards are usually inexpensively printed at a print shop so you will have plenty to use during your job search.

Some Uses for PIC Cards

○ **Attach one to a resume.**

○ **Attach them to completed applications.**

○ **Give them to friends or relatives. Ask them to keep you in mind if they hear of any job openings. And ask them to give the card to someone else who might know of a job.**

○ **Enclose one in your thank-you note after an interview or phone contact.**

○ **Give several to people who are willing to give them to others. Everyone you know should get a few. Ask them to give them to others who might know of a job opening for you.**

○ **Post them on bulletin boards in Laundromats, Grocery Stores, and other high-traffic areas.**

You may have other ideas on how to use them. The more you can put into circulation, the better!

GET THEM OUT THERE IF YOU WANT TO GET NOTICED!

The Layout of a PIC Card

There is more to a well-written PIC Card than you might first think. Examine the different sections of a PIC Card in the example below.

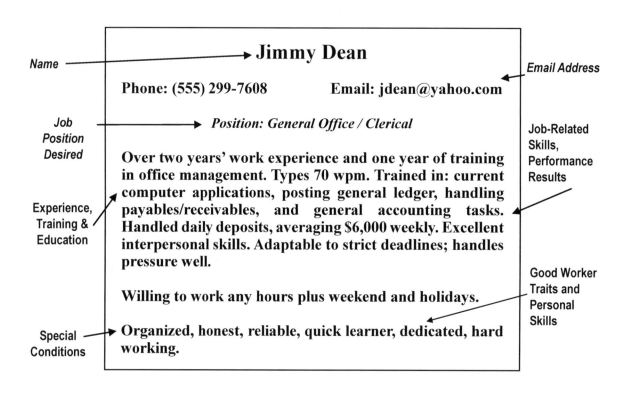

Note:
You will add other information specific to your PIC Card. The one above is just a sample. Just like you are an individual, your PIC Card will be individual to reflect your specific skill sets.

Tip:
You can use a 3"x5" index card for practice in class, but the finished product is a business card sized unit. Any local print shop can produce your PIC Cards, starting at $10 for 500-1,000 of them.

LESSON 6

RESUMES

Tips for Lesson:

❖ Using the examples and exercise sheet provided, along with any other available materials, have each student prepare a rough draft of a "Skills Resume."

❖ Review each student's rough draft as they do it. Be sure to have enough help so each person receives enough attention and specific help. This rough draft will be the foundation for the completed word-processed resume.

❖ Discuss cover letters and thank-you notes using the materials provided in the lesson section.

Resume Production

Get It Word Processed on a Computer
Make sure your resume looks professional. Using a computer and laser printer will produce the best-looking resume. This is the way most resumes are done.

If You Don't Have a Computer
If you are not experienced in using a computer seek professional assistance. Most small print shops and resume-writing services can produce a professional looking resume for a modest cost. Unless you need help in writing your resume, a one-page resume should cost no more than $50.

Make Plenty of Copies
While networking and using cold contacts, it is to your advantage to give each one of these contacts one or more copies of your resume. Plan to have lots of copies available. You may go through several hundred before you land your next job.

Use Quality Paper
Most print shops will have a supply of good quality papers and matching envelopes for use with resumes and cover letters. The best papers have a rich look and texture. They cost more, but are worth every penny. Ivory, white, and off-white are conservative colors that look professional. If you are on a fixed budget, ask your printer for discounted or discontinued stock. Use plain white paper only if you lack sufficient funds.

A Few Words on Resumes
Even the best of resumes will not get you a job. You will have to do that yourself. And, to do so, you will have to get interviews and do well in them. Interviews are where the job search action is, not resumes.

Don't Listen to Experts
If you ask ten people for advice on your resume, they will all be willing to give it—yet no two of them will agree. You will have to make up your own mind about your resume. Feel free to break any "rules" if you have a good reason for doing so. It's your resume. Don't avoid the job search by worrying about your resume. Write a simple and error-free resume, then go out and get lots of interviews. Later, you can write a better resume—if you want or need to.

How to Write Cover Letters

This type of letter was originally called a cover letter because it went along with, and "covered," a resume. Different situations need different types of letters. You may find that you don't need to send many formal letters. Many job seekers get by with informal thank-you notes sent with copies of resumes and PIC Cards. But certain types of jobs, and some organizations, require a more formal approach. Use your judgment. As always, make certain that all your job search correspondence makes a good impression.

❖ Send It to Someone By Name and Title
   o Find the name of the person who will most likely to supervise you. You should call first to set up an interview. Then send your letter and resume.

❖ Get Your Facts Straight
   o Make sure you get the person's name, organization name, and address correct. Include the person's job title.

❖ Be Friendly and Professional
   o A professional style is usually best. Avoid a "Hire me now!" approach. No one likes to be pushed. Still, make it clear that you are interested in starting right away.

❖ Be Clear about What You Want
   o If you want an interview, ask for one. If you are interested in that company or business, say so. Give clear reasons why they should consider hiring you.

❖ Make It Look Professional
   o As with resumes, any correspondence to prospective employers must look good. Use quality paper and matching envelopes. A standard business format is best for most letters.

❖ Qualify Your Letter
   o Reasons for sending a cover letter include: responding to an ad, asking an employer for an interview, and following up after a phone call or interview. Each of these letters will be different.

❖ Follow Up on Everything
   o Contacting an employer personally is much more effective than sending a letter. Don't expect letters to get you many interviews. They are best used to follow up after you have contacted the employer. *Remember: you never get a second chance to make a first impression!*

Thank You Notes

One of the most critical steps that often are overlooked by job candidates is to send a "thank-you note" after an interview. A written note will be added to your interview file. It will stick in the mind of the interviewer and will give you a last chance to create a good impression.

Several tips for writing thank-you notes:

- ❖ Keep it short but not too short. "Thanks a lot for the interview" isn't enough. Write something like, "I just wanted to thank you again for the opportunity to interview with you on Dec. 2. I enjoyed meeting you and the other members of your team to discuss the customer service position."

- ❖ Describe something specific that will place you solidly in the interviewer's memory.

- ❖ In the next paragraph, restate the skills and experience that make you the best applicant for the job.

- ❖ The note should be typed, with no spelling or grammatical errors, on quality paper.

- ❖ Don't wait more than 24 hours after an interview to send the note.

- ❖ In the last paragraph, express your enthusiasm for the job and your commitment to do your best.

- ❖ If you feel that you forgot to mention something critical in the interview, use your notes to find what you missed.

- ❖ Tell the interviewer that you will call in a few days to check on the status of your application. Always follow up on an interview even if you find another job. Never burn bridges when you don't have to.

Common "Key" Words
for Resumes

acquired	consulted	exchanged	issued	planned	scheduled
administered	contacted	exerted	judged	posted	secured
admitted	contracted	exhibited	justified	prepared	sent
advised	contrasted	experienced	kept	prescribed	separated
aided	controlled	expanded	learned	presented	served
allowed	converted	fabricated	lectured	priced	serviced
analyzed	convinced	facilitated	led	printed	set up
answered	coordinated	fed	licensed	processed	showed
applied	copied	figured	Listened	produced	sold
appointed	corrected	filed	listed	programmed	solicited
appraised	corresponded	filled	loaded	promoted	sorted
arranged	counseled	financed	located	prompted	stocked
assembled	counted	finished	logged	proofread	stored
assessed	created	fired	mailed	proposed	strived
assigned	debated	fitted	maintained	proved	summarized
assisted	decided	fixed	managed	provided	supervised
attached	delivered	formulated	manufactured	published	supplied
attended	demonstrated	founded	marked	purchased	tallied
authorized	deposited	governed	marketed	ran	taught
balanced	described	graded	measured	rated	tested
billed	designed	graphed	met	read	telephoned
bought	detailed	greeted	modified	rearranged	transferred
budgeted	determined	handled	monitored	rebuilt	transport
built	developed	headed	motivated	recalled	tutored
calculated	devised	helped	negotiated	received	typed
cashed	diagnosed	hired	nominated	recommended	verified
cataloged	discovered	identified	noted	reconciled	
changed	dismantled	implemented	notified	recorded	
charged	dispatched	improved	numbered	reduced	
charted	dispensed	improvised	observed	referred	
checked	displaced	increased	obtained	registered	
classified	directed	indexed	opened	regulated	
cleaned	distributed	indicated	operated	related	
cleared	documented	informed	ordered	relayed	
closed	drew	initiated	organized	renewed	
coded	drove	inspected	outlined	reorganized	
collected	earned	installed	overcame	repaired	
commanded	educated	instructed	packaged	replaced	
communicated	employed	insured	packed	reported	
compiled	encouraged	integrated	paid	requested	
completed	engineered	interpreted	participated	researched	

Sample Cover Letter

After An Interview

Joseph L. Chiappetta Jr.
PO Box 24-3664
Boynton Beach, FL 33424

April 10, 20XX

Sam and Janet Evening
Bali-Hi Production Corp.
227 N. Market Street
Atlanta, Georgia 21649

Dear Mr. and Mrs. Evening:

I know you have a busy schedule so I was pleasantly surprised when you arranged a time for me to see you. While you don't have a position open now, your organization is just the sort of place I would like to work in. As we discussed, I like to be busy with a variety of duties and the active pace I saw at your company is what I seek.

Your ideas on increasing business sound creative enough to work. I've thought about the customer service problem and would like to discuss with you a possible solution. It would involve the use of a simple system of color-coded files that would prioritize older correspondence to give them a priority status. The handling of complaints could also be speeded up through the use of simple form letters similar to those you mentioned. I have some thoughts on how this might be done too, and will work out a draft of procedures and sample letters if you are interested. It can be done on the computers your staff already has given me and will not require any additional costs to implement.

Whether or not you have a position for me in the future, I appreciate the time you have given me. An extra copy of my resume is enclosed for your files or to pass on to someone else.

Let me know if you want to discuss the ideas I presented earlier in the letter. I will call you next week as you suggested, keeping you informed of my progress.

Sincerely,

Joseph L. Chiappetta Jr.

Sample Resume

Joseph L. Chiappetta Jr.
PO Box 24-3664
Boynton Beach, FL 33424
joejr122@yahoo.com

Objective:
Seeking employment in the field of Information Technology and E-Commerce. Prefer a job with numerous challenges that will allow me to use and develop my skills. I will be a great asset to any organization that hires me and be loyal to any business that gives me an opportunity to prove my worth.

Education:
- ❖ High School Diplomas—State of Arizona and State of Florida
- ❖ Micro Computer Concepts—Central Arizona College
- ❖ Professional Development Certification—Department of Homeland Security
- ❖ Thirty Two (32) Federal Emergency Management Certifications—FEMA
- ❖ Small Business & Entrepreneurial Certification—Central Arizona College
- ❖ Business Management—Ashworth College

Experience:
Central Arizona College, Florence, Arizona—Approx. 2 years
I have held positions as College Clerk, Teacher's Aide, and Programs Facilitator for Computer Concepts and Transitional Living. I was also responsible for preparing lessons, scheduling classes, and keeping detailed records of all activities.

Western Historical R&D Inc., Clearwater, Florida—Approx. 10 years
I was Vice President of Operations and supervised all research projects for the company. Helped create the company as a manager and promoted from within to an executive position.

Skills:
- ❖ Competent with Computer technology and Skilled with Many Current Programs
- ❖ Online and Telephone Sales: Incoming and Outgoing
- ❖ Extensive Business Management and Clerical Skills
- ❖ Extensive Knowledge in the Use of Various Chemicals and Compounds
- ❖ Excellent Driver with No Accidents or Citations for over Fifteen (15) Years

Personal:
I am reliable, a creative problem solver, and self-motivated. I approach my work with diligence and great pride, and I am willing to go the extra mile to get the job done right the first time. I have my own transportation, and I am willing to work flexible hours. I have had a great variety of experiences and work that make me an asset to any company.

References:
Jeanne C. Reynolds, Founding Director, Gold Canyon Heart & Home, 602.555.1212
Michael Iovino, Security Consultant, Former ADC Chief of Security, 520.555.4646

(Sample PIC Card)

Joseph L. Chiappetta Jr.
joejr122@yahoo.com

Skills:

Competent with Computer technology and Skilled with Many Current Programs, Online and Telephone Sales: Incoming and Outgoing, Extensive Business Management and Clerical Skills, Perform well with Challenging Tasks, Able to Meet Deadlines, Organized and Punctual, Excellent Driver with No Accidents or Citations for over Fifteen (15) Years

Personal:

Reliable, a creative problem solver, self-motivated. I approach my work with diligence and great pride; willing to go the extra mile to get the job done right the first time. I have my own transportation, and I am willing to work flexible hours. I have had a great variety of experiences and work that make me an asset to any company.

Resume Worksheet

- -

Name: _____

Address: _____

Home Phone: _____

Cell Phone: _____

Email: _____

EMPLOYMENT OBJECTIVE

_____

_____

EDUCATION:

_____ Graduated: _____

_____ Graduated: _____

_____ Graduated: _____

WORK EXPERIENCE

Company Name: _____ Duration: _____

Address: _____ Phone: _____

Job: _____

_____

_____

Company Name: _____ Duration: _____

Address: _____ Phone: _____

Job: _____

_____

_____

SKILLS AND QUALIFICATIONS:

_____

_____

_____

_____

PERSONAL STATEMENT:

_____

_____

_____

_____

REFERENCES:

_____

_____

_____

Explaining the Employment Gaps On My Resume

With the number of unemployed Americans now in the millions, finding a job can be a daunting task. Job seekers have to make themselves stand out in a crowd of possibly thousands of applicants just to get an interview. Then, when the seemingly impossible interview date has come, the applicant has another set of touch questions to answer.

One of the hardest things that applicants have to explain is the dreaded employment gap. Many employers want to know just what you've been doing between jobs and the answer to this question can make or break an interview. Here are some ideas that have been provide by individuals who have used them and proven them to be effective.

Re-charge Your Batteries

Several years ago, I took off an entire summer to spend time with my family. I have a long, stable work history and I made sure to point this out to potential employers upon returning to the workforce. I explained that my sons were entering their teenage years and would soon be too big to spend time with Dad. This accomplished two things for me. First, it demonstrated to the potential employers that my family was old enough to not be an issue with my career. The second thing it did was allow me to explain to the employer that I was re-energized and ready to move forward with my career goals.

Brush Up On Your Skills

More recently, I was laid off as a member of management of a nationally franchised restaurant company. While laid off, I immediately took classes to enhance my PC skills. Being in finance, it's important to have a well-rounded knowledge of financial systems, so I took the opportunity to take some certification classes in different billing and financial systems. I make very clear to prospective employers that I didn't simply sit around and watch courtroom shows and soap operas.

In addition to this, I have had some applicants tell me that they have taken various free Microsoft classes offered through the local unemployment offices. This demonstrated to me that this applicant was a go-getter that would help out in different areas when called upon as opposed to someone who'll simply sit around and wait to be told what to do.

The Entrepreneur

One potential employee showed the zest and energy that I was looking for by going after an idea he had been toying with for years. The applicant explained that when he was laid off, he took that time as an opportunity to attempt to launch his own business.

Saying this is easy, but this applicant thoroughly explained the time and effort he put into making his idea come to life. Even though the attempted business idea turned out to be a failure, it demonstrated to me that this guy was a worker who would put in the extra effort when needed.

Don't Wait For the Interview

When you have an employment gap on your resume, the employers see it long before the interview. Knowing this, why would you want to wait for the interview to explain it?

A cover letter is a perfect place to explain a gap in employment. Not only have I used this, but I've seen it done by applicants time and time again. I've seen thorough explanations that covered gaps caused by layoffs to caring for terminally ill family members.

If emailing your resume, be sure to take the time to explain these gaps in the body of the email as well as by pointing out the explanation in your cover letter. Attention to detail like this stands out in the minds of an employer and can be the difference between getting the interview and getting your resume deleted.

Showcase Marketable Skills in your Resume Skills Section

Have you thought about the skills you're listing in your résumé's Skills section? If you treat this section as an afterthought, you could be missing an opportunity to show employers you've got the right skills for the job. When completing the Skills section, consider the skills important to the job you're seeking. The best way to get started is to search job titles on Monster.com and review postings for your target job. Look at the ideal requirements in the ads and write a list of frequently repeated skills. Next, create a list of your matching skills that you can incorporate in your resume. Keep in mind you develop skills in everything from work experience to education and training, hobbies, extracurricular activities, volunteer work, and even self-study.

Three Types of Skills

❖ Job-Related: Relevant to a specific job. For example, an accountant's job-related skills might include financial planning, budgeting and financial reporting.
❖ Transferable: Skills learned in one field or job that are applicable to different ones are transferable. These skills can reflect how you deal with things (assembly, machine operation), data (research) and people (instruct, manage and negotiate).
❖ Adaptive: These skills are the hardest to substantiate as they include personality traits and characteristics that determine your work style. Adaptive skills include reliability, ability to get along with colleagues, honesty and productivity.

Adding Your Skills to Your Resume

Job-related and transferable skills are the most desirable to list on your resume. For each skill, indicate your skill level and years of experience. It's important to be honest when describing your skill level. While it's tempting to deem yourself an expert, once you get the interview or job, you may need to prove your claim. But this is not the place for modesty either; call yourself fan expert if you are truly at that level.

Here's a guideline for rating your skill level:

❖ Beginner: A novice understanding of the skill. You have exposure to the sill and understand its basic concepts but lack experience.

- ❖ Intermediate: Between a beginner and an expert. You have experience with and can carry out the skill but don't understand its advanced concepts.
- ❖ Expert: A highly developed skill level. You have solid experience and training with the skill and understand advanced concepts. You demonstrate superior skills.

How Many Skills to List?

Employers quickly scan resumes, so long lists are not likely to get read. Instead, select 10 to 15 of your strongest, most desirable skills. A short, targeted skills list will be more effective than one that's long and overwhelming.

Refreshing your resume doesn't need to be painful. Your efforts could pay off with big dividends. Arm yourself with an updated, high-octane resume, and this could be the year that you land a better job. Now is a great time to reflect on your recent accomplishments and add them to your resume. Here are some ideas to help guide you.

Find Your Passion

Make sure your resume instantly communicates your career target with a descriptive headline (e.g., "CPA Backed by Corporate Audit Experience") and adequately reflects your depth and breadth of experience in a brief, hard-hitting opening summary highlighting your top selling points.

If you're thinking about changing careers or industries, be sure you've clearly defined you goal. Your job search will be more successful if your resume targets a specific filed instead of being a one-size-fits-all document. Research positions to gain a solid understanding of what you want to do as well as the qualifications employers are seeking. Once you identify your career target, assess your background and identify transferable skills and experience that will enable success. Add a resume objective that spells out your goals and shows relevance of past experience. For example: "Award-winning educator seeking to leverage five years teaching experience to transition into corporate training."

Add New Employment, Skills and Accomplishments

Refreshing your resume also means keeping it current. If you've changed jobs during the past year, earned a promotion or expanded responsibilities, your resume should reflect this. Even if you've remained in the same position, you've probably achieved noteworthy accomplishments in the last year. Don't forget about your new skills, including technical and computer ones. Add your new skills to the Skills section on Monster's Resume Builder. Survey your Skills section to ensure your proficiency level and years of experience are current.

Keep Keywords Up-to-Date

Study job postings on Monster that match your career target, and not which keywords appear repeatedly. Incorporate keywords that match your background into your resume.

Include New Professional Activities

Add professional-development activities you completed last year, including certificates, degrees, courses and in-service training. Also include professional organizations you've joined and industry conferences you've attended. List training programs you've begun, even if you haven't completed them. This shows your commitment to ongoing professional development.

Edit Ruthlessly

As you add new information to your resume, also consider the usefulness of older or less relevant experience. This will ensure your resume doesn't become unwieldy. Unless you want to return to a former career, decrease the amount of detail you provide for older experience. For job seekers with 10 years of experience or more, this may mean setting up an Early Career section, where you briefly summarize employers, job titles and employment dates. Other expendable items include obsolete technology and your high school diploma once you've earned a college degree. Proofread your resume carefully to ensure it is error-free. Watch for information that needs to be updated from previous versions. For example, if your old resume included a summary that stated your years of experience, increase this number if necessary.

Start a Kudos File

Resolve to start a file for projects and successes you achieve during the year. Copy performance reviews and keep them in this file. Print out complimentary or congratulatory emails and file these away. List new committees you join. Jot down assignments you complete during the year. Include details of quantifiable results (e.g., percentages, dollar amounts, before/after comparisons) of your efforts while still fresh in your mind. Your kudos file will remind you where you excelled so you'll be ready to punch up your resume.

Update Regularly

You should refresh your resume throughout the year, not just at the beginning. You never know when opportunity may come knocking.

The Biggest Resume Mistake You Can Make

Your resume is the most important document in any job search. But what if you're submitting resume after resume and receiving no results at all? Your resume may be fatally flawed. How can a resume betray a job seeker? It's not just typos or poor formatting. "The biggest flaw for a resume is when it fails to showcase a person's accomplishments, contributions and results, and instead spouts a job description of each position he's held," says Lauren Milligan, founder of ResuMayDay, a resume-writing and career-coaching firm based near Chicago.

1. Think Big

Whatever jobs you've held—be it as an assistant or a CEO—think beyond the everyday tasks of your position. "People get bogged down in the day-to-day details of their jobs, but when it comes to your resume, you've got to get out of the clutter and ask yourself, 'What does this work mean?'" Milligan says.

2. Be Clear

Focusing on accomplishments rather than specific responsibilities will help keep your resume concise. "There's a huge difference between a resume and the Great American Novel," says Milligan. "The resumes I'm most proud of summed up a 25-year career in a single page." Remember that resumes are typically skimmed for a mere 6-8 seconds. "Make sure you're identifying the companies you worked for, how long you were there and if you earned a promotion," she says. "Those are things that people look for immediately." If your job title is long and vague, tighten it up so people immediately understand what you've done. For example, "Marketing Manager" is much more accessible than "Global Identity Architect." Given the time you have to catch a recruiter's eye, a focused, accomplishment-driven resume is the way to go. "If you are loaded up on peripheral stuff, it's too hard for a hiring manager to find your story," Milligan says.

3. Get Real

What if you come up blank when trying to think about how you've helped build the big picture for your employer? "A couple of times I've talked to people who insisted they just did their jobs and there's nothing special about them that jumps out," Milligan says. She's asked them outright if they're in the right position. "It's a difficult question to ask, but these people may be chasing the wrong job," she says. She counsels clients that if they cannot speak about what they've done in terms of enhancing the position or the company, "You may be just punching a clock—and you and your employer deserved more." Look for other opportunities in which you can contribute and grow professionally. You'll enjoy a more rewarding career and have a more successful resume.

LESSON 7

APPLICATIONS
AND
INTERVIEWS

Tips for Lesson:

Using the sample application provided, go over the proper methods for filling out a job application. (10 minutes) Be sure to point out basics such as:

- ❖ All capital letters
- ❖ Correct spelling
- ❖ Neatly printed handwriting
- ❖ Never leave blank spaces
- ❖ Proper use of "N/A" (not applicable) in spaces where information is not required or not applicable. (10 minutes)
- ❖ Honesty and accuracy are stressed. NEVER lie on an application!

Go over each student's application with the entire class. (20 minutes)
Discuss the interview process as it relates to the job application to prepare students for the next lessons. (10 minutes)

Sample Job Application

Date: _____

Application For Employment
(PLEASE PRINT ALL REQUESTED INFORMATION IN INK)

We are an Equal Opportunity Employer and do not discriminate against any individual in any phase of employment in accordance with the requirements of local, state, and federal law. In addition, we adopted an Affirmative Action Program with the goal of ensuring equitable representation of qualified women, minorities, Vietnam Era, and disabled veterans, and other disabled individuals at all job levels.

Applicants may be subject to testing for illegal drugs. In addition, applicants for certain positions that receive a conditional offer of employment must pass a medical examination or meet other criteria prior to receiving a confirmed offer of employment.

PERSONAL INFORMATION

LAST NAME	FIRST NAME	MIDDLE INITIAL	SOCIAL SECURITY NO.

STREET ADDRESS OR RFD NO. (include apartment number, if any) | HOW LONG AT THIS ADDRESS:

CITY	STATE/PROVINCE	COUNTY/PARISH	ZIP CODE

HOME PHONE (include area code)	WORK PHONE (include area code) Ext.	SEX (for statistics only) ☐ Male ☐ Female	Other Last Names ever used

PREVIOUS ADDRESS (if less than one year) | HOW LONG AT THIS ADDRESS?

CITY	STATE/PROVINCE	COUNTY/PARISH	ZIP CODE

POSITION APPLIED FOR:

I AM AVAILABLE FOR: ☐ Part-time   ☐ Full-time
Complete the Hours Available for Work chart below

HOW DID YOU HEAR OF THIS OPENING?

	Sun.	Mon.	Tues.	Wed.	Thurs.	Fri.	Sat.
LOWEST RATE OF PAY YOU WILL EXCEPT — From:							
To:							

WHEN WILL YOU BE AVAILABLE FOR WORK (month and year)	ARE YOU AVAILABLE FOR TEMPORARY EMPLOYMENT?	YES	NO
	A. less than 1 month..		
IF HIRED, CAN YOU FURNISH PROOF OF AGE? ☐ YES ☐ NO	B. 1 to 4 months..		
	C. 5 to 12 months...		

Answer the following only if the position for which you are applying requires driving.
Are you licensed to drive a car?   ☐ Yes   ☐ No
Is license valid in this state?   ☐ Yes   ☐ No

HAVE YOU EVER BEEN BONDED?   ☐ NO   ☐ YES—When?

DO YOU HAVE ANY PHYSICAL HANDICAPS PREVENTING YOU FROM DOING CERTAIN TYPES OF WORK?
☐ NO   ☐ YES—If yes, describe the handicap/limitation?

HAVE YOU HAD ANY SERIOUS ILLNESS IN THE PAST 5 YEARS?   ☐ NO   ☐ YES   If yes, describe

Please list any special skills, training or experiences, which qualify you for the position, which you are applying.

Please list any additional qualifications and skills (skills with machines, patents, or inventions, your most important publication [do not submit copies unless requested] your public speaking and publications experience, membership in professional or scientific societies, etc.)

Kind of license or certificate (pilot, registered nurse, lawyer, radio operator, CPA, etc.)	Latest license or certificate:	Approximate words per minute:

EDUCATION

Did you graduate from high school or will you graduate within the next nine months, or do you have a GED high school equivalency certificate? ☐ YES (month, year) ☐ No, highest grade completed	Name and location (city and state) of last high school attended

Name and location (city, state, ZIP code, if known) of college or university. (If you expect to graduate within the next nine months give MONTH and YEAR you expect to receive your degree).	Dates Attended		No. of Credits Completed		Type of Degree (e.g. B.A.)	Year of Degree	GPA
	From	To	Semester Hours	Quarter Hours			

Chief undergraduate college subjects:	No. of Credits Completed		Chief graduate college subjects:	No. of Credits Completed	
	Semester	Quarter		Semester	Quarter

Major field of study at highest level of college work:

Other schools or training (for example, trade, vocational, Armed Forces or business). Give for each the name and location (city, state, ZIP code, if known) of school, dates attended, subjects studied, number of classroom hours of instruction per week, certificate, and any other pertinent data.
_____
_____

Activities, honors, awards, and fellowships received:

Languages other than English. List the languages (other than English) in which you are proficient and indicate your level of proficiency by putting an (X) in the appropriate columns.

	PROFICIENCY							
	Can Prepare and Deliver Lectures		Can Converse		Have Facility to Translate Articles, Tech. Materials, etc.		Can Read Articles, Technical Materials, for Own Use	
Name of Language	Fluently	With Difficulty	Fluently	Passably	Into English	From English	Easily	With Difficulty

REFERENCES

List three persons who are NOT related to you and have definite knowledge of your qualifications and fitness for the position for which you are applying. Do not repeat names of supervisors listed under EXPERIENCE.

Full Name	Present Business or Home Address (Number, Street, City, State, and ZIP Code)	Telephone Number (include Area Code)	Business or Occupation

NOTE: a conviction or a firing does not necessarily mean you cannot be appointed. The circumstances of the occurrence(s) and how long ago it (they) occurred are important. Give all the facts so that a decision can be made.

	YES	NO
1. Within the last five years have you been fired from any job for any reason?...		
2. Within the last five years have you quit a job after being notified you would be fired?...		

If your answer to questions 1 and 2 is "YES", give details in the space provided on the following page. Show the name and address (included ZIP Code) of employer, approximate date, and reasons for each case. This information should agree with your answers under EXPERIENCE.

	YES	NO
3. Have you ever been convicted, forfeited collateral, or are you now under charges for any felony or any firearms or explosives offense against the law? A felony is defined as any offense punishable by imprisonment for a term exceeding one year, but does not include any offense under the laws of a state as a misdemeanor...		
4. During the past seven years, have you been convicted, imprisoned, on probation or parole, or forfeited collateral, or are you now under charges for any offense against the law not included in the above question?...		

NOTE: When answering the previous two questions, you may omit (1) traffic fines for which you paid $100.00 or less, (2) any offense committed before your 18th birthday which was finally adjudicated in a juvenile court or under a youth offender law, (3) any conviction the record of which has been expunged under federal or state law, and (4) any conviction set aside under the Federal Youth Corrections Act or similar state authority.

	NAME	ADDRESS	RELATIONSHIP	PHONE NUMBER
PERSONAL REFERENCES				

LIST ONLY PERSONS WE MAY CONTACT—BE SURE TO INCLUDE PHONE NUMBER

	YES	NO
5. While in the military service, were you ever convicted by a general court-martial?............................. If your answer to questions 3, 4, or 5 is "YES", give details in the space below. Show for each offense, (1) date; (2) charge; (3) place; (4) court; (5) action taken.		
6. Do you receive, or do you have pending, application for retirement or retainer pay, pension, or other compensation based upon military, federal, civilian, or District of Columbia government service?........... If your answer to this question is "YES", give details below. If military retired pay, include the rank at which you retired.		

Your statement cannot be processed until you have answered all questions, including questions 1 through 6 above.

QUESTION #	SPACE FOR DETAILED ANSWERS. BE SURE TO INDICATE QUESTION NUMBER TO WHICH THE ANSWERS APPLY.

If more space is required, use full sheets of paper approximately the same size as this page. Write on each sheet your name, birth date, and announcement or position title. Attach all sheets to this page.

VETERAN PREFERENCES

Answer all parts. If a part does not apply to you, answer "No".

	YES	NO
Have you ever served on active duty in the United States military service? (Exclude tours of active duty for training in the Reserve or National Guard)..		
Have you ever been discharged from the armed services under other than honorable conditions? (You may omit any such discharge changed to honorable or general by a Discharge Review Board or similar authority)................		

If the above answer is "YES", you will be required to furnish records to support your claim at the time you are hired. List dates, branch, and serial number of all active service (enter NA, if not applicable)

FROM	TO	BRANCH OF SERVICE	SERIAL OR SERVICE NUMBER	

BRANCH	RANK	DUTIES	SALARY FROM	TO	REASON FOR CHANGE IN RANK

List any special school or skills acquired during your military service:

EXPERIENCE

Begin your current or most recent job or voluntary experience and work back. Account for periods of unemployment exceeding three months and your residence address at that time on the last line of the experience blocks in order of occurrence.

May inquiry be made of your present employer regarding your character qualifications and record of employment   ☐ YES   ☐ NO

1. NAME AND ADDRESS OF EMPLOYERS ORGANIZATION

Dates employed (month/year)		Average number of hours per week	Salary or Earnings	
From	To		Start $	per
			End $	per

Exact title of your position	Name of immediate Supervisor	Area Code Phone number	Number and kind of employees you supervised

Kind of business or organization (manufacturing, accounting, social services, etc.)

Reason for Leaving

Description of work (describe your specific duties, responsibilities, and accomplishments in this job.)

_____
_____
_____
_____

2. NAME AND ADDRESS OF EMPLOYERS ORGANIZATION

Dates employed (month/year)		Average number of hours per week	Salary or Earnings	
From	To		Start $	per
			End $	per

Exact title of your position	Name of immediate Supervisor	Area Code Phone number	Number and kind of employees you supervised

Kind of business or organization (manufacturing, accounting, social services, etc.)

Reason for Leaving

Description of work (describe your specific duties, responsibilities, and accomplishments in this job.)

_____
_____
_____
_____

3. NAME AND ADDRESS OF EMPLOYERS ORGANIZATION

Dates employed (month/year)		Average number of hours per week	Salary or Earnings	
From	To		Start $	per
			End $	per

Exact title of your position	Name of immediate Supervisor	Area Code Phone number	Number and kind of employees you supervised

Kind of business or organization (manufacturing, accounting, social services, etc.)

Reason for Leaving

Description of work (describe your specific duties, responsibilities, and accomplishments in this job.)

_____
_____
_____
_____

Filling Out Job Applications

Disclosing a Felony Conviction

It is especially important for ex-offenders to be truthful in filling out applications. However, the truth must be told in a way for the offender to get screened-in and invited to a face-to-face interview.

Question:

"Have you ever been convicted of a felony?"   × Yes   ☐ No

If yes, please explain: "Will explain at interview; I can be bonded."

Below are some compelling reasons to answer the question in this way.

- ❖ It allows you to be honest, yet protects your privacy by controlling who knows about the specific details of your conviction.
- ❖ Stating the felony is not job related and the applicant is bondable may help calm the fears of the employer and perhaps even pique his/her curiosity enough to decide to interview you. Remember, being able to successfully defuse the fear people have surrounding knowing about your crime may lead to employment.
- ❖ All Community Supervision Officers will tell an employer if you have a felony.
- ❖ It is better that an employer find out about your crime from you. That way you control the flow of information—how it's worded, how it's presented.
- ❖ Virtually all employers do background checks—you *will* be found out.
- ❖ In the interview, you can talk about how productive you were in prison or jail and about the transferable skills you developed participating through institutional programming.
- ❖ Employers can take advantage of Tax Credits and bonding.

Below is a list of other options to answering this questions and probable consequences.

- ❖ Check 'YES' and write the conviction. The candidate would likely be screened out and would lose privacy because anyone in the office who saw the application would know about the conviction.
- ❖ Leave the question blank and/or put N/A. The application would appear incomplete and it would appear the applicant is hiding something. When disclosing the felony at the interview, it would be awkward to explain why the questions are not filled in truthfully.

Consequences:

What if you check 'NO' and lie? This appears to be the easiest route and may help you get a job for the short term, but the long-term consequences may destroy short-term gain. Consequences include:

- ❖ Not being hired because the lie was found out.
- ❖ Being fired as soon as the background check comes back . . . and it WILL.
- ❖ Carrying around emotional baggage wondering when you will be found out.
- ❖ Reinforcing ex-offender stereotypes.
- ❖ Prosecution—especially if offender applied for a federal job.

Most employers do background checks before employers are promoted. So if an offender lied on the application, stayed with the company for a few years, became eligible for promotion, and the lie was exposed, the offender could:

- ❖ Lose a good job.
- ❖ Lose a good reference.
- ❖ Lose financial stability.
- ❖ Lose self-esteem.

Question:

"Have you been convicted of a crime within the past ten years that directly relates to the position for which you are applying?" ☐ Yes ☐ No

- ❖ If the crime you have been convicted of has no direct relationship to the position for which you are applying you may answer "no". However, if the answer is "yes" you should mark "yes".

Example: You were convicted of forgery, and you are applying for a job as a bank teller. You would answer "yes" because your conviction has a direct relationship to the bank teller position.

Question:

What should I write if the question about conviction asks me to "explain"?

- ❖ Always write "will explain at interview". This will keep everyone who may view your application from knowing your personal business.

Question:
How do I cover time in prison or jail on the "Work Experience" portion of the application?

❖ List only 2 or 3 of the jobs that may be in line with your future employment goals. If you did any work during your incarceration (teacher's aide, cook, clerk, janitor, firefighter, etc.) submit the jobs where you gained significant hands-on experience. Choose the jobs that best describe and reflect skills gained, abilities developed, and accomplishments earned.

Example: If you worked both in food services and in maintenance while incarcerated, you would indicate both jobs for your incarceration period and list only the year for dates of employment even though you may have moved from facility to facility and from job to job.

Question:
How do I complete the "business name"?

❖ Use the abbreviated name of jail or corrections facility.

Question:
What about completing the "address" portion of Job History?

❖ Do not use P.O. Boxes. Use only the city and state as the address, or only list the street address of the institution. The reason is that some people associate P.O. Boxes with prison or jail in certain towns.

Question:
What about phone numbers for previous employers?

❖ Obtain permission to list your last work supervisor's direct contact phone number. If you don't know it, research it; write a letter for the phone number and request permission from the person responsible who oversaw your work or duties. If it's not possible to obtain a direct phone number to an individual, list the main phone number of the facility, or as a last resort list "unknown" as the contact phone number. If previous private employers are no longer in business, state that as the phone number. Collecting accurate phone numbers is important to make it easy for the employer to verify past jobs. It it's too difficult, the employer may get frustrated and bypass the rest of your application, moving to the next one.

Question:
How to complete the "reason for leaving" portion of Work Experience?

❖ Correct responses can be "relocated," "contract ended," "transferred," or "pursued other opportunities".

This is an example of a Work Experience Response. The reason for completing the Work Experience portion this way is to get your application past whoever may be screening applications. It is vital that your work experience is complete; yet don't advertise your incarceration. That information is only between you and the interviewer, not anyone who may see your application.

References

References are people you know who can tell employers about who you are and what you can do. References confirm the information on your employment application and/or resume. They also support your character, skills, accomplishments, and work habits. Having good things said about you from another person is reassuring to the employer. Ask permission before listing a person as a reference. Ask your references for their business cards to have all their correct contact information.

Types of References

Who you choose to ask to be listed as references depends upon your experiences, job goals, and the position you're seeking. If you are an experienced worker use these references:

❖ Previous employers and supervisors
❖ People you may have supervised
❖ Former fellow workers

If you are a job hunter re-entering the work force use these references:

❖ Members or leaders of groups you belong to (community, religious groups, etc.)
❖ Supervisors from a part-time or full-time job
❖ Teachers

If you are looking for your first real job use these types of references:

❖ Personal friends
❖ Counselors
❖ Doctors, teachers, lawyers

LESSON 8

INTERVIEW PRACTICE

Tips for Lesson:

❖ Students are given various materials from the book and any other available resources.

❖ Discussion of interview basics and the importance of hygiene, posture, eye contact, and effective speaking are all gone over in great detail.

❖ Practice involves group and individual mock interviews taking place. Students take turns role-playing both applicant and employer in front of the entire class.

❖ At the end of this lesson the Federal Bonding Program, Tax Credits, and One Stop Career Centers are discussed in detail.

The Power of Handshakes

There actually is a secret handshake . . .

And the "secret" is actually well known among communications experts who study body languages and nonverbal communication. In business settings, the handshake that defines confidence, sincerity and openness goes like this: Right hand extended and vertical, a firm but not a crushing grip, and in Texas, three or four full pumps up and down. On the East Coast, it's three to five shorter, quicker pumps. In California, it's just one or two quick pumps—anything more than that is just too much. So says communications specialist Patti Wood, who trains business people and public speakers on improving their presentation skills, and who frequently interprets the body language of the rich and powerful for the media. "It's not the firmness so much as the fact that the palm of your hand has full contact with the palm of the other person's hand," Wood says. She argues that it takes 90 seconds for someone to form an opinion about another person based on first impressions. In business whether it's a making sales pitch, building clientele or creating rapport with co-workers, bosses or employees, those first 90 seconds are crucial and hard to erase.

Elissa Foster, communications professor at the University of Texas at San Antonio, agrees. "It's hard to swallow that 95 percent of what we understand of a person or a message is communicated nonverbally," Foster said. "But when you think about what is being communicated with the tone of the voice, clarity and color of the tone, the pausing and pitch, and the articulation, all of those come through the voice. And just like with the body, the tone of voice can be difficult to control unconsciously, which is why we pay attention those things." You can script what you say, but it's harder to control how you say it. If someone is saying they are trustworthy, but they're not looking you in the eye, or they're making a strange face, you become suspicious. The formal study of body language and nonverbal communication began in earnest during the 1950s, with the publication of "Introduction to Kinesics," written by Ray Birdwhistell. Since then, several books have been written about hand movements, intercultural nonverbal communication, and something called "Paralinguistics," or the study of the voice. Perhaps the most accessible of texts includes the recently published "Field Guide to Gestures: How to Identify and Interpret Every Gesture Known to Man," by Nancy Armstrong and Melissa Wagner. Like apes and bears, the powerful and those aspiring for power try to dominate a social interaction by taking up as much space as possible, broadening their shoulders, standing with their feet apart, or sitting with their legs spread out. When shaking hands, some try to dominate that interaction by forcing his or her hand on top in a horizontal position, rather than a vertical, equal position. Others try to dominate by squeezing harder than necessary.

"You can never take one gesture or one eye movement or posture and say this means that," Foster said. "One of the things with nonverbal communication is that it is notoriously ambiguous. If people try to read other people and assume that they know because they've done a one-to-one translation, you're on the wrong track. Nonverbal communication can mean a lot of different things." Nevertheless, people often make quick assumptions because of how they've interpreted nonverbal cues. And in important situations, such as job interviews, people rely on their interpretations of body language.

"Most hiring decisions are made within the first 10 seconds of a meeting, before you even sit and talk," Wood said. "No matter what a person says after those 10 seconds, the interviewer spends their time saying to themselves, 'I was right,' looking for information to confirm their first impression." Wood advises job candidates to smile sincerely as they give a firm and formal equal-power handshake, both at the beginning and the closing of an interview. "Because even if you don't think you did well, you want to face that person, smile and give them a good handshake," she said. "You can save a bad interview with a good handshake." Once on the job, workers join an increasingly diverse workplace with plenty of room for misinterpretations of nonverbal cues. A hand on another person's shoulder can read as a fatherly gesture, a patronizing move, or a sexual advance. A failure to look a person in the eye can be viewed as a cue to deception, when for others it could be a sign of respect or timidity.

When you're not sure about what a touch or a look means, Foster and Wood both say the best course of action is to talk about it.

"You can do a perception check and say, 'Well, every time you come to my desk, you lay your hand on my shoulder. Are you trying to be reassuring, or are you trying to say something else?'" Foster said. Explicit communication, being explicit is the best thing to do, but it can be tough.

Wood said that in tricky male-female workplace interactions, women would tend to give off nonverbal cues if they're uncomfortable with a set of sexual jokes or a way of touching. Men, she said will typically not pick up on those cues.

"Most of the time," Wood, said, "When women tell men to stop telling jokes or touching, they stop."

Women will say, "He should have known I was upset because I was letting him know with my body language," but people don't necessarily read that nonverbal language," Wood said. "Since some people don't read that nonverbal language, you have to be the one to talk about it."

The Ins and Outs of Providing References
From U.S. News & World Report

You've likely been asked for references in an interview or during the application process. Rather than scrambling to pull a few together, you should have these all prepared well in advance and keep the reference information in one place.

❖ Step 1: Create a Separate Document

You shouldn't include references in your resume. You don't want to risk a recruiter or hiring manger reaching out to your references prematurely or without permission. Instead, guard your references' time and contact information as if it were your own. Fielding too many calls could make them think twice about offering their experiences working with you. To avoid this, keep your references noted on a separate document and send them along only when asked.

❖ Step 2: Ask Your Contacts

Always ask your contacts if it's okay to use them as references before giving their information to potential employers. It certainly would be awkward if you listed a reference who didn't feel comfortable recommending you. People don't like to be caught by surprise, and they need time to think back to the time they worked with you to give accurate information.

Your reference list might not just include past supervisors; look to teachers, co-workers or junior employees you've managed. Skip the personal references unless you are specifically asked for them. A professional reference can attest to both your character and your work dedication.

❖ Step 3: Get Complete Contact Information

Some hiring managers prefer to call references, while others will simply ask a few questions via email. Make sure you give comprehensive contact information, including email and phone number. For business references, it is best to give out only business contact information—don't give their home phone numbers. You should note the details of your relationship (boss, colleague, direct report) with a reference, and the company where you worked together, so the hiring manager or recruiter can decide which people are most relevant.

❖ Step 4: Customize

Each prospective employer may look for something different in different types of references (personal, professional, co-worker, boss), so be sure to include contacts that fit their request.

Make a master list of 10 or more potential references from your file of colleagues, bosses, direct reports, clients, and personal acquaintances. When it's time to prepare your references, give your potential employer three to five of the most relevant.

As time passes, you'll want to update your list of contacts who have worked with you more recently. A boss you had 10 years ago may not remember you well enough to give a strong reference, let alone be able to speak on your performance. Recent references from your past two jobs is standard.

Also make sure the contact information you have is still accurate each time you send it out. For example, your former boss may no longer work with the same company. Be sure to find out before you give erroneous contact information to a potential employer.

It's always nice to give a heads-up to the people on your list when you send the references, to let them know that they may be contacted and so that they can prepare to take the call.

Do Employers Really Check References?

Most of the time, yes. Sometimes it's enough that you are able to provide a list of contacts that would vouch for you. Some employers go on Google to see what they can discover about you. It's wise to search for yourself to see what pops up.

As a backup, you may want to include a character reference letter with your application. This is a letter written by a former boss that speaks to your abilities and skills. Not every hiring manager will ask for one, but it's always a good idea to keep a generically written reference on file just in case. After leaving a job—on good terms—ask your boss to write you a letter that you can use with any job application.

Personal Strengths

The following is a list of qualities that employers will look for you to demonstrate in your resume or during an interview. Choose the two or three qualities that you feel are the strongest in relation to the job for which you are applying and complete the statements below.

__ACCURATE	__DISCIPLINED	__MOTIVATED
__AMBITIOUS	__EFFICIENT	__NEAT
__ARTICULATE	__ENERGETIC	__OPEN-MINDED
__ASSERTIVE	__ENTERPRISING	__ORGANIZED
__CAREFUL	__ENTHUSIASTIC	__OUTGOING
__COMMITTED	__FLEXIBLE	__PATIENT
__CONFIDENT	__FRIENDLY	__POSITIVE
__CONSCIENTOUS	__GOAL-ORIENTED	__PRODUCTIVE
__CONSIDERATE	__HONEST	__PROFESSIONAL
__CONSISTENT	__HUMOROUS	__QUICK
__CREATIVE	__INDEPENDENT	__RESPONSIBLE
__DECISIVE	__INSIGHTFUL	__SKILLFUL
__DEDICATED	__KNOWLEDGEABLE	__STRONG
__DEPENDABLE	__A LEADER	__THOUROUGH
__DILIGENT	__LOYAL	__TOLERANT

Example:

I am thorough. I have shown I have this quality by: having a balanced register every day for two years when I worked as a cashier for Target Stores. This quality is important in my field because employers value someone whom they can trust and count on.

I am _____.

I have shown I have this quality by:

_____

This quality is important in my field because:

_____

10 Workplace Habits That Could Cost You Your Career

Experts agree that in the current employment climate, bad behavior is becoming less and less something employers tolerate—and more of a fireable offense. "For every one of you, there are 100 people lining up to take your job," says Kiki Weingarten, an executive career coach based in New York City. "Employers are more able than ever to be as picky as they want."

Here, four leading career coaches offer 10 bad workplace habits they've seen that send employees down the road to poor reviews. Check yourself before you wreck yourself.

Habit: You're addicted to email

In meetings, with clients, with your boss, you just can't stop scrolling through your BlackBerry. You think you're being productive by makings sure you don't miss a message while stuck in the weekly sales meeting but your colleagues (particularly those speaking) see it as a personal insult. Constantly checking your smart phone conveys a real sense of arrogance.

How to break it:

Put the BlackBerry down, especially if you're in a meeting. Turn it off, put it away, and leave it in your office. If you're waiting for a particular time-sensitive email, let your coworkers know beforehand.

Habit: You're a brown-noser

Nobody likes a kiss-up, and in the office one too many well-placed compliments could leave you with this reviled reputation. Say yes to everything a higher-up requests, and your coworkers can resent your enthusiasm. Even worse, your boss may see through your tactics and see you as more nuisance than team member.

How to break it:

Take a look at the last 10 thing you've said yes to, whether opinions or tasks around the office. When viewed honestly, is there anything you actually disagree with? Learning to say no from time to time shows your supervisor and your coworkers that you have backbone.

Habit: You're a busy-body

Do you mind your own business, or is your ear constantly perked for the latest office gossip? Your habit of needing to be in the know is likely a source of stress for your coworkers. Making everything and everyone your business is a recipe for disaster.

How to break it:

If it's information necessary to your position, schedule regular meetings with coworkers to stay abreast of current events. Otherwise, wait for information to come to you and avoid the tendency to jump into overheard conversations. As a last resort, invest in some headphones.

Habit: Your email etiquette is lacking

If your outbox reads more like a firing squad than friendly exchanges, it may be time to take a look at your communication style. Email has no tone, emotions, intonation, so it's easy for your short emails to be perceived as pushy, demanding, or impatient.

How to break it:

If poor email habits persist, bad feelings are bound to brew in the office. Read your emails again before you send them to gauge how they might be received, particularly if they're directed to someone outside of your office.

Habit: You're full of excuses

You may have forgotten your presentation notes, but you're not about to admit it. You don't know the answer to a question, yet you try to talk your way around it. The result is that you've wasted not only your time, but that of everyone around you.

How to break it:

Set a reminder 10 minutes before the start of every meeting, to give you a chance to prepare all the items you'll need. If you don't know an answer, admit it. Own up to your mistakes.

Habit: You're a multi-tasking mess

Technology has made multi-tasking the norm in most workplaces, but experts say it's causing more harm than productivity. If you've been caught more than once missing pertinent information in emails or correspondence—especially deadlines, dollar sings or project elements—it might be a sign you're not as skilled at juggling tasks as you think.

How to break it:

Make a conscious effort to focus on only the task in front of you. Read each email thoroughly and respond before moving on to the next. The habit of juggling different tasks is hard to break, but if your performance is suffering, the break must occur.

Habit: You're a prima donna

"That's not in my job description." The problem with setting too many boundaries at work, whether it's saying no to tasks or assignments you feel aren't your responsibility, or keeping ironclad 9-5 hours, is that when you think "self-protective", your coworkers think "jerk". Keep this attitude and you'll quickly find you've done yourself no favors by sticking to your guns. Chances are it's not in their job description either.

How to break it:

The next time an unattractive task comes across your desk, ask yourself who'll have to tackle it if you pass it off. Recognize that in periods of downsizing, everyone must pick up extra slack—your reputation will suffer if you make yourself the exception.

Habit: You're the office thief

If pens that are not yours keep "appearing" on your desk, chances are you have a "borrowing" problem. Walking off with people's pens, staplers, or coffee mugs is never going to win you any love.

How to break it:

Label your won things, or stick to a certain, identifiable brand. That way, the second you see an item on your desk that isn't your brand, you'll make a conscious effort to remember whose it is—and return it.

Habit: Your style does you no favors

Personal style is one thing, questionable style is another. When your supervisor questions whether your look is "client-appropriate" you've got a fashion-work conflict that could cost you your next promotion.

How to break it:

Imagine the closet of the person you admire most at the office. How do they dress, and why does it suit their position in the company? Imagine their daily wardrobe decision. Then go shopping with your role model in mind.

Habit: You're quick-tempered

An angry employee is a dangerous employee. Managers are wary of employees who are quick to anger. They know what 'going postal' means. If your blood pressure spikes every time the copier breaks down, or assistants scatter when you enter a room, it's time to reexamine your behavior. Uneasy or uncomfortable coworkers are unlikely to sing your praises.

How to break it:

To lose the reputation of a loose cannon, make an effort to pause before reacting to a stressful situation. Close your office door and take several deep breaths. By all means, avoid venting at coworkers before thinking it through. If all else fails, seek counseling. Chances are, you're angry about more than just the job.

The Federal Bonding Program
A Unique Job Placement Tool

Answers to Questions about Fidelity Bonding

- ❖ What Is It?
- ❖ Why Is It Needed?
- ❖ Who Is Eligible?
- ❖ How Is It Issued?
- ❖ Has It Had Success?

SPONSORED BY THE U.S. DEPARTMENT OF LABOR
For Further Information:
Contact RON RUBBIN at 1-800-233-2258 or www.bonds4jobs.com

What is Fidelity Bonding?

- ❖ Insurance Covering Employee Dishonesty
- ❖ Guarantee for Worker "Job Honesty"
- ❖ Employer Gets Free Bond: Job-Hire Incentive
- ❖ Program Bonds Any "At-Risk" Applicant
- ❖ Eliminates Bonding As Employment Barrier
- ❖ Employer Gets Skills Without Taking Risk

Users of Bonding Services

- ❖ One-Stop Career Centers
- ❖ Welfare-to-Work Programs
- ❖ Offender Placement Centers
- ❖ State Labor Exchange Offices
- ❖ WIA Service Deliverers
- ❖ Non-Profit Organizations

Federal Bonding Program
Q&A

Q. What Proof Is There That Bonding Is Needed and Useful?

A. New York State found that having a job helps prevent a parolee from returning to prison. The fact is that 89% of persons who violated parole were unemployed at the time. Texas found that Project RIO bonding and other services for releases from its State prisons saved the State $10 million annually, and made taxpayers out of tax users. A study of the U.S. Department of Justice found that released felony offenders with histories of alcohol and drug offenses could be helped to secure steady employment by offering employers bonding as a job-hire incentive. In August 1998, the Pittsburgh City Paper brought attention to the fact that "a criminal past may prevent the transition from welfare to work," and called for expanded use of the Federal Bonding Program to deal with this job placement problem.

Q. Are There Other Benefits In Use Of Bonding Services?

A. YES. A greater variety of jobs can be obtained by applicants, and more higher-wage jobs can be obtained.

Q. Who Must Request Issuance Of The Fidelity Bond?

A. Issuance of the bond for job placement to occur can be requested by either the employer or the job applicant. This request is to be made to the local agency certified by the Federal Bonding Program. Any agency assisting job seekers can acquire bonds.

Q. Can The Bond Be Issued At Any Time?

A. For the bond to be issued, the employer must make the applicant a job offer and set a date for the individual to start work. The job start date will be the effective date of the bond insurance, which will terminate six months later. After the six months, continued coverage will be made available for purchase if the worker has exhibited job honesty under the program's bond.

Q. How Much Bond Insurance Coverage Will Be Issued?

A. A total of $5,000 bond coverage is usually issued, with NO DEDUCTIBLE for the employer. Larger bond amounts can possibly be issued under certain circumstances.

Q. What Papers Must The Employer Sign And What Other Actions Must The Employer Take In Order To Get The Bond?

A. NONE. Once the date is set for the applicant to start work, the bond can be issued instantly. The employer signs NO papers, and keeps NO special records since the bond is self-terminating. The bond is mailed directly to the employer by The McLaughlin Company in Washington, DC as agent for Travelers.

Q. Since Employers Buy Fidelity Bond Insurance To Protect Against Employee Dishonesty, Why Is The Program's Bond Needed?

A. Fidelity Bonds that employers purchase commercially do not cover anyone who has already committed "a fraudulent or dishonest act." Ex-offenders and other job applicants with questionable backgrounds are designated by the insurance industry as being NOT BONDABLE because they are too risky to insure for job honesty. Only the Federal Bonding Program will issue bonds to employers to cover anyone who is usually NOT BONDABLE. As a result, bonding is eliminated as a barrier to employment and the program serves as a unique job placement tool.

Q. Is It Legal for Employers to Deny Employment To Applicants Who Are NOT BONDABLE Under Commercially Purchased Bonds?

A. Employers fear that applicants who are NOT BONDABLE will be untrustworthy employees and companies can require bonding and deny employment on that basis. The Federal Bonding Program can help overcome that employer fear by making the applicant BONDABLE. The program's bond is like a guarantee of employee job honesty for the hardest-to-place job applicants.

Q. Can the Program's Fidelity Bond Coverage Exist Forever?

A. The key purpose of the program's bond is to help an at-risk applicant get a job. The bond insurance is issued free-of-charge to the employer for a period of six months. If the worker demonstrates job honesty during the six months of Federal Bonding Program coverage, that worker can become BONDABLE FOR LIFE under commercial bonding made available to the employer for purchase from the Travelers Property Casualty insurance company.

Q. Can Bonding Be Issued For A Worker Placed On A Part-Time or Temporary Job?

A. Usually, bonding is issued to cover workers who obtain permanent jobs providing at least 30 hours work per week. However, the agency issuing the bond can make an exception to this rule if they determine it is needed.

Q. If an Applicant Is to Be Placed on a Job Where Bonding Was Not Previously Required, Can a Bond be Issued?

A. YES. Bonding can be provided for any job if issuance of the bond is the difference between getting the job and not getting it. Job placement often occurs simply due to the fact that the bond overcomes an employer's fear that the job applicant may be a dishonest worker.

Q. Can Bonding Be Issued To Cover An Already Employed Worker?

A. The main purpose of the Federal Bonding Program is to help secure employment for applicants who are having a hard time getting a job due their questionable backgrounds. However, a bond can be issued to cover a current employee who is NOT BONDABLE under the employer's insurance, and needs the program's bonding in order to secure a promotion to a new job requiring bonding or to prevent being laid off.

Q. Is A Person On Welfare Automatically Eligible For Bonding?

A. Most welfare recipients will be eligible due to the fact that have a poor credit history or have declared bankruptcy. Also, some of these individuals will be eligible due to being ex-offenders or ex-addicts or to their lack of a work history.

Q. What Is The Federal Bonding Program?

A. It is a unique tool to help a job applicant get and keep a job. The program issues Fidelity Bonds, and is sponsored by the U.S. Department of Labor.

Q. What Is A Fidelity Bond?

A. It is a business insurance policy that protects the employer in case of any loss of money or property due to employee dishonesty. It is like a "guarantee" to the employer that the person hired will be an honest worker. The Fidelity Bonds issued under the Federal Bonding Program are insurance policies of the Travelers Property Casualty Insurance Company. The McLaughlin Company in Washington, DC, is the agent for Travelers in managing the program nationwide.

Q. How Does The Bond Help Someone Get A Job?

A. The bond is given to the employer free-of-charge, and serves as an incentive to the company to hire a job applicant who is an ex-offender or has some other "risk" factor in their personal background. The employer is then able to get the worker's skills without taking any risk of worker dishonesty on the job.

Q. What Exactly Does the Bond Insurance Cover?

A. It insures the employer for any type of stealing by theft, forgery, larceny or embezzlement. It does not cover liability due to poor workmanship, job injuries or work accidents. It is not a bail bond or court bond for the legal system. It is not a contract bond, performance bond or license bond sometimes needed to be self-employed.

Q. How Can You Know If You Qualify for Obtaining Bonding Services?

A. Anyone who cannot get a job without bonding is eligible for help by the Federal Bonding Program. All individuals who have, in the past, committed a fraudulent or dishonest act, are eligible for bonding services. These persons include ex-offenders and ex-addicts, as well as people who have poor personal credit, poor persons who lack a work history, and individuals who were dishonorably discharged from the military.

Q. At What Age Can You Obtain Bonding From The Program?

A. You must meet the legal minimum working age set by the State in which the job exists. The program has no maximum age limit.

Q. What If You Have Already Been Told By A Company That You Are "NOT BONDABLE"?

A. The main reason that the Federal Bonding Program exists is to help get a job for any person who experiences bonding as a barrier to getting a job. The program will bond anyone who has been told (or will be told) that they are NOT BONDABLE.

Q. Can The Program Bond Persons Who Are Self-Employed?

A. NO. The program's fidelity bond is issued to an employer to cover only a worker who earns wages with Federal taxes automatically withheld from the worker's paycheck.

Q. What Restrictions Exist In The Program's Bond Coverage?

A. The worker must meet the State's legal age for working; there are no age limits. The job usually is to be for at least 30 hours work per week. Workers must be paid wages with Federal taxes automatically deducted from pay; self-employed persons cannot be covered.

Q. Who Does The Program Help?

A. Bond coverage is provided for any person whose background usually leads employers to question their honesty and deny them a job. The program will cover any person who is a "risk" due to their being in one or more of the following groups:

- ❖ Ex-offender with a record of arrest, conviction or imprisonment; anyone who has ever been on parole or probation, or has any police record.

- ❖ Substance abusers who are being rehabilitated through treatment for alcohol or drug abuse, poor credit record, or have declared bankruptcy.

- ❖ Dishonorably discharged from the military.

- ❖ Persons lacking a work history who are from families with low income.

Targeted Jobs Tax Credit

This program exists in all 50 states under several different names. These Tax Credit programs offer employers a credit against their tax liability for hiring individuals from nine target groups who have traditionally had difficulty obtaining and holding jobs. For most target groups' employers may claim a credit of 40% of the first year's wages up to $6000 per employee. Employers are allowed a maximum credit of $2400 per employee the first year. A minimum employment period of 90 days or 120 hours is necessary before the employer can claim the tax credit. Paperwork is minimal. Employees must be registered for the program. This voucher must be delivered to a Department of Economic Security Job Service office or the Program Unit or postmarked on or before the fifth day after the individual begins work. Otherwise the employer must request program certification in writing on or before the start date. This request must be delivered to a Department of Economic Security Job Service office or the Program Unit or postmarked on or before the start date.

$2,400 for Hiring an Ex-Felon
Internal Revenue Service
1111 Constitution Avenue, NW
Washington, DC 20224
202-622-6080 and 800-829-1040 (Business Tax Questions)
www.irs.ustreas.gov/formspubs/index.html

(Work Opportunity Tax Credit-Ex-Felon)
For each Ex-Felon hired by the employer who is a member of a low-income family, a tax credit of up to $2,400 (40% of first year wages) is available under the Work Opportunity Tax Credit. All new adult employees must work a minimum of 120 or 400 hours. The tax credit is $750 for 120 hours, $1,200 for 400 hours. To apply for certification, employers must: 1) Complete IRS Form 8850, Pre-screening Notice and Certification Request for the Work Opportunity and Welfare-to-Work Tax Credits, by the date the job offer is made; 2) Complete either the ETA Form 9062, Conditional Certification Form, if it is provided by the job seeker, or ETA Form 9061, Individual Characteristics form, if the job seeker has not received a Conditional Certification; and 3) mail the signed and dated IRS and ETA forms to their State Employment Security Agency / State Workforce Agency/ WOTC/WTW Coordinator. The IRS 8850 Form must be mailed within 21 days after the new hire's employment start date. Copies of IRS forms are available from your local IRS office or the IRS website listed above. To order forms by phone, call 800-829-3676; to order by fax, call 703-368-9694. ETA Forms and a listing of coordinators are available through Fax-on-Demand at 877-828-2050 or from the Department of Labor website at www.uses.doleta.gov/wotcdata.cfm.

The Human Equation
In Hiring Ex-Offenders

I want to share an experience with you. Sometimes it comes down to the human equation when dealing with people who are ex-offenders and employers alike. We like to think that employer incentives, background checks and great resumes are the key to employment for ex-offenders but when all is said and done, it is the human equation that is most important.

I was at a meeting some time back when one of these incredible events took place. I was meeting with a new employer who had contacted me in regards to hiring ex-offenders. At that meeting, the Human Resource Director and two other executives for this company were present. One of the executives wanted to make sure that if we sent ex-offenders we did not send sex offenders or any violent criminals. I stated that I understood why sex offenders were on his list, but asked if his company could accept some violent offenses. I asked if some violent offense could be made an exception to the rule, and he agreed that some, if committed over a period of sever or more years ago, could be accepted. He then stated that any offense that involved murder or a weapon was out of the question.

I prefaced this story so you would have some idea of what the atmosphere in that meeting was like prior to the remainder of this story. I also need to tell you that, prior to this meeting, I had invited a client of mine to come and apply for a job with this employer. I did this without knowing the employer's stand on violent offenders. The client in question had a conviction for 2nd degree murder.

At the meeting, before the client arrived, I told the prospective employers of the crime. I told them he had spent many years in prison for the crime and that he had done a great deal to change his life for the positive. I also told them that in prison he was a model inmate. All of this did little to dissuade the executive.

In a few minutes the receptionist came in to inform us that my client had arrived. He was invited in. The employer who had the objection to hiring violent felons asked my client about his crime. My client did not try to excuse his actions, but was informative and took accountability. He went on to tell the employers that it was not easy to walk the straight path in prison. He was constantly on trial for his commitment to getting out with something to show for his time. He went on to tell of all the classes and schooling he was involved in and how he worked hard to make changes in his life.

I saw a change in the attitude of the executive. He went from very judgmental about this person and his crime to a sense of respect and understanding.

I am leaving out details for a reason. I want to protect this employer and client from being embarrassed.

Nevertheless, I need to tell you that I was amazed! This employer went from being adamant about not hiring violent ex-offenders to offering this man a job.

All of this was the result of an ambassador, my client. He did all of the right things. He did not make excuses for his behavior, but instead told the employer all of the events that demonstrated his change and commitment to being crime free.

I left that meeting with a sense of hope, and I know the executive changed the way he looks at ex-offenders. This was not the result of my work or of programs and incentives; this was the result of an ex-offender changing the way one person looked at violent felonies.

This was the result of an ex-offender doing the right thing, taking responsibility for his actions, and showing a history of change while in prison.

"It is the human equation."

From a letter written by: Steven B. Temple GCDF

Ex-Offenders and Felons can Increase Their Chances of Getting Hired

Written by Eric Mayo

The goal of most ex-offenders, after leaving the criminal justice system, is to find a job. The key to remaining free and getting the most out of life for ex-offenders and felons is finding stable employment. Studies have shown that ex-offenders that have steady employment are far less likely to re-offend.

One of the tough realities is that criminal records are there to stay. They aren't going anywhere. There are people who will hold criminal pasts against them. There is a bright side to this situation. Many employers are willing to hire competent people from any source. Good employees are hard to find. Among the growing untapped labor sources in the country are those who are classified as "ex-offenders" or "ex-felons".

Employers are finding that giving ex-offenders and felons an opportunity makes good economic sense. Individuals who were incarcerated but are committed to overcoming the past make excellent employees. Most are self-disciplined, hardworking, and dependable.

Many employers take advantage of the Work Opportunity Tax Credit. The Work Opportunity Tax Credit (WOTC) encourages the employing of individuals who are members of target groups, by providing a federal tax credit incentive of up to $9,000 for employers who hire them. Included in these target groups are ex-offenders. You can get more information about the WOTC at www.doleta. gov/business/Incentives/opptax/.

The key to finding a job is having a definite plan. Job seekers are about to begin a marketing plan designed to sell a product. The product is their set of skills and attitude. They must be able to let prospective employers know what they can do and how it can work for them. The ability to identify and describe skills gives them an advantage. They must then find employers that can use their skills. Finding a job is a numbers game. The more job leads, the more interviews. The more interviews, the more offers. The challenge is to get as many leads as possible. The interview is the time where the product is matched to the employer's needs. To get a job, one must sell oneself through proper appearance, presentation of qualifications and poise. The applicant must make the employer feel that they are right for the job. Preparation is key. Have the right wardrobe, develop a well-written resume and practice face-to-face interviews. Especially be prepared to answer difficult questions regarding past employment and criminal history.

Getting a job with a criminal record is not an exact science but one can increase the odds by being prepared. Good luck!

Interview Tips

The primary idea of an interview is to share information. It is your chance to sell the employer on the concept that you are the best person for the job. To be completely prepared, here are some tips to remember before, during, and after the interview.

Before

- ❖ Research the company, the job, the salary range, and the interview.
- ❖ Do your homework; write answers to the questions that might be asked.
- ❖ Prepared questions to ask the interviewer.
- ❖ Have a copy of your resume ready.
- ❖ Develop and prepare your Personal Career Portfolio to take with you.
- ❖ Take time for good grooming and hygiene.
- ❖ Go alone and plan to arrive at least 15 minutes early.
- ❖ Prepare your thank-you cards prior to the interview.
- ❖ Visit job site prior to interview to determine location, parking, and travel time.

During

- ❖ Do not chew gum or smoke.
- ❖ Relax, be yourself, and demonstrate self-confidence.
- ❖ Maintain eye contact with the interviewer.
- ❖ Demonstrate good posture and mannerisms.
- ❖ Be enthusiastic.
- ❖ Stress you qualities and skills.
- ❖ Don't speak unkindly of a former employer or former teacher.
- ❖ Keep a businesslike attitude.
- ❖ Ask questions about the job or company.
- ❖ Do not ask about salary until you have been offered the job.

After

- ❖ Thank the interviewer for his/her time; smile and shake hands.
- ❖ Thank the receptionist for his/her courtesy, and ask for the interviewer's business card for the thank-you card.
- ❖ Send a thank-you card within 24 hours of the interview.
- ❖ Once you have been offered a job, you can negotiate salary.

Interview Questions / Answers

1. Tell me about yourself...
    a. Where you're from, family situation, and your hobbies / interests
    b. Describe your previous work experience / training / education
    c. Summarize your skills

2. Why are you looking for this sort of job? Why here?
    a. Enjoy this type of work, and have passion for it
    b. I am very impressed with this company and the way it is managed
    c. Good company to grow with, and further advance in this field

3. How does your previous experience relate to this job?
    a. My prior work experience includes most of the skills that are required for this position
    b. My job related skills are transferable and can directly improve this company's performance
    c. My prior work experience has taught me how to work well with others, and as team player

4. Why should I hire you?
    a. Explain how your skills & abilities can specifically help their business to run better
    b. Dependable, honest, and trustworthy
    c. Good social skills / work well with others
    d. Quick learner and can easily be taught new skills
    e. Able to effectively adapt to a new work environment

5. What are your strengths?
    a. Explain job related skills, personal traits, and people skills
    b. Work smart and use creativity to solve problems
    c. Complete the job right the first time, can meet deadlines and excel under pressure
    d. Follow instructions well and can work unsupervised
    e. Self motivated, self starter, and able to encourage other to perform better

6. What are your weaknesses?
    a. Everybody has something they can improve upon
    b. I try to overcome weaknesses as I become aware of them
    c. I feel that I have no weaknesses that will prevent me from doing this job

7. Tell me about your personal situation . . . (felony conviction)
    a. Explain that you were young and everyone makes mistakes
    b. Describe what positive accomplishments you've had since then
    c. Explain how this experience has changed your life for the better

8. What are your plans for the future?
    a. Grow roots in the community
    b. Raise a family, providing stability and support
    c. Grow in my career, continue training and education, and hopefully advance in this company

9. What will your former employers / references say about you?
    a. Only positive things
    b. Reliable & honest
    c. Willing to learn and grow

10. What sort of pay do you expect to receive?
    a. Pay is negotiable
    b. As with any professional, 1 want to be paid my true value
    c. I know I can benefit your company, and once I prove this to you I would expect a raise.

Answering Embarrassing Questions

Q. Why should I hire you?

This is where you sum up your qualifications, what you have to offer the employer, and your best "bottom line" sales pitch. Never humiliate yourself, but don't be afraid to ask for what you want.

Q. Why did you commit your crime?

That's a tough one. Be honest. Tell them what happened, what was going on in your life at that time, and how you've grown beyond that experience.

Q. How do I know you won't break any more laws?

Explain your desire not to go back to prison. Many taking this course will be under some kind of supervision when they're applying for a job. Use this supervision to your advantage. Explain that there's nothing more important to you than staying out and that being supervised means that the employer has someone to call if there's a problem. If it truly is your desire to stay out, then this should not cause you any concern at all, but may encourage your employer.

Q. What was prison like?

Again, be honest and direct. Most people don't have a clue what you have survived. Spin this into a positive rather than a negative. Talk about all that you have learned, any classes or jobs you held, and also emphasize that you were using that time to better yourself.

Tips for the Interview

❖ Shower and shave before you go.
❖ Keep your hair neat.
❖ Do not wear a beard.
❖ Brush your teeth and use mouthwash.
❖ Trim your fingernails and clean them.
❖ Never chew gum.
❖ Never bring anyone with you.

❖ Use deodorant.
❖ No goatee or van dyke.
❖ Trim your mustache.
❖ Avoid long sideburns.
❖ Cover your tattoos.
❖ Never smoke.
❖ Never swear.

Some Things that Offend Employers

- Poor personal appearance
- Lack of enthusiasm
- Vise-grip handshake
- Tardiness/Late for interview
- Evasive answers to questions
- Know-it-all or superior attitude
- Sloppy writing/Lazy attitude
- Bad remarks from former employers
- Poor eye contact
- Limp handshake
- Lack of job-related questions
- Overly aggressive or conceited
- Failure to express gratitude
- Low morals

Major Issues for Employers

The following are qualities that most employers want to see in their applicants. Try to put yourself in the employer's shoes and ask yourself what you expect from somebody who wants to work for you.

- Management Potential

  - This individual is someone who will be around for 5 years from now. A foresighted person who takes a genuine interest in the company and knows the business as well as his supervisor does: a problem solver and a leader. Someone who will get the job done but still gets along and works well with others.

- Trustworthiness

  - This individual is someone who can be left alone with the cash register and inventory or equipment. This is a person who the employer can rely upon to tell him the truth, regardless of the circumstances. Somebody the supervisor or owner can confide in and talk to without worrying that the topic will be spread around the workplace.

10 Tips to Boost Your Interview Skills

Even the smartest and most qualified job seekers need to prepare for job interviews. Why, you ask? Interviewing is a learned skill, and there are no second chances to make a great first impression. So study these 10 strategies to enhance your interview skills.

Practice Good Nonverbal Communication

It's about demonstrating confidence: standing straight, making eye contact and connecting with a good, firm handshake. That first nonverbal impression can be a great beginning—or quick ending—to your interview.

Dress for the Job or Company

Today's casual dress codes do not give you permission to dress as "they" do when you interview. It is important to know what to wear to an interview and to be well groomed. Whether you wear a suit or something less formal depends on the company culture and the position you are seeking. If possible, call to find out about the company dress code before the interview.

Listen

From the very beginning of the interview, your interviewer is giving you information, either directly or indirectly. If you are not hearing it, you are missing a major opportunity, good communication skills include listening and letting the person know you heard what was said. Observe your interviewer, and match that style and pace.

Don't Talk Too Much

Telling the interviewer more than he needs to know could be a fatal mistake. When you have not prepared ahead of time, you may ramble when answering interview questions, sometimes talking yourself right out of the job. Prepare for the interview by reading through the job posting, matching your skills with the position's requirement and relating only that information.

Don't Be Too Familiar

The interview is a professional meeting to talk business. This is not about making a new friend. Your level of familiarity should mimic the interviewer's demeanor. It is important to bring energy and enthusiasm to the interview and to ask questions, but do not overstep your place as a candidate looking for a job.

Use Appropriate Language

It's a given that you should use professional language during the interview. Be aware of any inappropriate slang words or references to age, race, religion, politics or sexual orientation—these topics could send you out the door very quickly.

Don't Be Cocky

Attitude plays a key role in your interview success. There is a fine balance between confidence, professionalism and modesty. Even if you're putting on a performance to demonstrate your ability, overconfidence is as bad, if not worse, as being too reserved.

Take Care to Answer the Questions

When interviewers ask for an example of a time when you did something, they are asking behavioral interview questions, designed to elicit a sample of your past behavior. If you don't give an example, you not only don't answer the question, but you also miss an opportunity to prove your ability and talk about your skills.

Ask Questions

When asked if they have any questions, most candidates answer, "No". Wrong answer. You should be ready to ask questions that demonstrate an interest in what goes on in the company. Asking questions also gives you the opportunity to find out if this is the right place for you. The best questions come from listening to what you're asked during the interview and asking for additional information.

Don't Appear Desperate

When you interview with the "please, please hire me" approach, you appear desperate and less confident. Maintain the three Cs during the interview: cool, calm and confident. You know you can do the job; make sure the interviewer believes you can, too.

50 More Questions

Here is a list of 50 interview questions. It came from a survey of 92 companies who interviewed college students for jobs after graduation. Most of the questions are those asked of any adult. Look for the questions you would have trouble answering. These are the ones you need to practice answering! In doing so, re-member to use the three-step process . . .

A List of Questions Often Asked by Employers

1. In what school activities have you participated? Why? Which do you enjoy the most?
2. How do you spend your spare time? What are your hobbies?
3. Why do you think you might like to work for our company?
4. What jobs have you held? How were they obtained, and why did you leave?
5. What courses did you like best? Least? Why?
6. Why did you choose your particular field of work?
7. What percentage of your school expense did you earn? How?
8. What do you know about our company?
9. Do you feel that you have received good General training?
10. What qualifications do you have that make you feel that you will be successful in your field?
11. What are your ideas on salary?
12. If you were starting school all over again, what Courses would you take?
13. Can you forget your education and start from Scratch?
14. How much money do you hope to earn at age 25? 30? 40?
15. Why did you decide to go to the school you attended?
16. What was your rank in your graduating class in high school? Other schools?
17. Do you think that your extracurricular activities were worth the time you devoted to them? Why?
18. What personal characteristics are necessary for success in your chosen field?
19. Why do you think you would like this particular type of job?
20. Are you looking for a permanent or temporary job?
21. Are you primarily interested in making money or do you feel that service to your fellow human beings is a satisfactory accomplishment?
22. Do you prefer working with others or by yourself?
23. Can you take instructions without feeling upset?
24. Tell me a story!
25. What have you learned from some of the jobs You have held?
26. Can you get recommendations from previous employers?
27. What interests you about our product or service?
28. What was your record in the military service?
29. What do you know about opportunities in the field in which you are trained?
30. How long do you expect to work?
31. Have you ever had any difficulty getting along with fellow students and faculty? Fellow workers?
32. Which of your school years was most difficult?
33. Do you like routine work?
34. Do you like regular work?
35. What is your major weakness?
36. Define cooperation.
37. Will you fight to get ahead?
38. Do you have an analytical mind?
39. Are you willing to go where the company sends You?
40. What job in our company would you choose if You were entirely free to do so?
41. Have you plans for further education?
42. What jobs have you enjoyed the most? The least? Why?
43. What are your own special abilities?
44. What job in our company do you want to work toward?
45. Would you prefer a large or a small company? Why?
46. How do you feel about overtime work?
47. What kind of work interests you?
48. Do you think that grades should be considered by employers?
49. Are you interested in research?
50. What have you done that shows initiative and willingness to work?

Answering Questions About A Criminal Record

The most difficult question you will be asked in an interview is the one about a criminal record.

❖ Be honest and forthcoming. Give the information that the interviewer asks for—no more, no less. It is important to maintain eye contact with the interviewer, so that he or she will know you are sincere.

❖ Briefly explain. Explain what was going through your mind at the time, and what was troubling you. Take responsibility for your actions. Don't make excuses. Admit what you did was wrong. If people were hurt by your actions, express your regret and describe any amends you have made to them or to their families.

❖ Talk about what you have learned from your mistakes. Discuss your insights, maturity, or wisdom you have gained. Talk about how your values have become clear as a result of your prison experience. Be specific. What are your values now? What were your insights? Explain why this experience makes you a good choice: having grown wiser from the experience and becoming a better person.

Describe ways that you have changed your life. For example, refer to any volunteer work or community organizations you've been involved with. Or if you've been clean and sober for a good while now, you could say that. But don't take too long. You don't want to spend a lot of time on the subject of your past.

❖ Get on with the interview. As soon as you feel you've said all you need to say and your interviewer seems satisfied, it's time to change the subject back to the job and the company, maybe with one of your own questions.

It is certain that you will have to talk about your prison record at some point. In fact, it's probably best if you bring it up first. You might say, "You may have noticed on my application that I wrote I'd been in prison. I'd like to quickly explain about that if you don't mind."

Never bring up the subject of your conviction at the beginning of the interview, and never wait until the end, either. Always bring it up in the middle of the interview, after you have expressed enthusiasm for the job and sold your accomplishments.

Questions about Drugs and Alcohol

If you were arrested for drugs, or if you have a history of drug abuse, you will have to explain. You could say you've been in treatment for this problem (if you have been) and/or that you've been religiously attending 12-step meetings and have been clean and sober for quite a while now (if you have been). You could also express your willingness to submit to drug tests for however long the employer thinks is necessary. Be sincere. Speak from the heart about where you've been with this problem and where you are now. But again, don't get too involved! Don't take long. This shouldn't be the main topic of your interview!

Sample Outline for Disclosing Felony Convictions and Prison Sentences

❖ There is something you have the right to know:

❖ In (year) _____ , I was convicted of _____ .

❖ At the time my judgment was clouded by _____ .

❖ I admit that this was a serious error in my judgment and I want to assure you that I have changed.

❖ I worked while I was incarcerated as a _____ and learned how to:

❖ There are some advantages you are eligible for if you decide to hire me.

○ I can be bonded up to $50,000.

○ As an employer, you are eligible for a Tax Credit Program and be eligible to receive up to a $2,400 federal credit for the first $6,000 of my wages.

❖ I am aware that my past actions may cause you to question my judgment, but I am prepared to do whatever it takes to proved myself to be a reliable and capable employee.

The trick to answering questions regarding incarceration is to "TELL THE TRUTH!"
Accept responsibility for what you did: "I can't blame anyone other than myself for what I did." Limit the amount of details you provide: "I know; it sounds simple, but there is not much more to it than that." Explain how this event improved your life as a learning experience.

What Can an Employer Ask About My Incarceration?

Almost everyone has some interest in knowing about the "darker side" of life. The same may be true of interviewers. They're interested in an "inside view" of prison life.

❖ Indicate lack of fun: "I'm sure you understand that prison is not a place where most people want to be."

❖ Simply state what a "working day" in prison is like. "I had to wake up at 5:30 each morning, if I wanted to eat. Then I prepared for work. After that, it was pretty much like any other job. I had to meet the production quotas, do good work and follow the directions of the supervisors . . . or else I didn't get paid or wasn't allowed to stay on the job."

❖ Relate prison employment to competitive work: "In fact, a day at work in prison is not too much different than a workday on the outside."

Prospective employers can inquire about arrests; whether charges are still pending, have been dismissed, or led to conviction of a crime involving behavior which would adversely affect job performance. Inquiries concerning convictions or imprisonment will be considered to be justified by business necessity if the crimes inquired about relate reasonably to the job duties, and such convictions (or release from prison or jail) occurred within the last ten years.

NOTE: Don't let the employer drag you into talking in detail or at length about what goes on in an institution. That is not the purpose of your interview session.

❖ Keep your answers simple and clear (evasive responses sound like you're hiding things or lying . . .)

❖ Keep you answers brief.

❖ Keep your dignity.

9 Common Interview Questions That are Actually Illegal

During job interviews, employers will try to gather as much information about you as possible, so there's bound to be some questions that will require you to think.

But it's the simple questions that are often most harmful, and even illegal. Any questions that reveal your age, race, national origin, gender, religion, marital status and sexual orientation are off limits.

"If you look at the broad picture, the [interview] questions you're asked have to be job related and to about who you are as a person," says Lori Adelson, a labor and employment attorney and partner with law firm Arnstein & Lehr. If you are asked any inappropriate questions, Adelson advises not to lie, but, instead, politely decline to answer. "Could they not give you a job because of that? Sure," Adelson says. "But if they do, they would be doing exactly what they're not supposed to do.

Here are some illegal interview questions that are often mistaken as appropriate and judicial.

Have you ever been arrested?

An employer can't actually legally ask you about your arrest record, but they can ask if you've ever been convicted of a crime. Depending on the state, a conviction record shouldn't automatically disqualify you for employment unless it substantially relates to your job. For example, if you've been convicted of statutory rape and you're applying for a teaching position, you probably won't get the job.

Are you married?

Although the interviewer may ask you this question to see how much time you'd be able to commit to your job, it's illegal because it reveals your marital status and can also reveal your sexual orientation.

Do you have children?

Again, the employer may ask you this question to see your available time commitment with the company, but this question is inappropriate. However, they are allowed to ask you directly if you have other responsibilities or commitments that will be conflicting to your work schedule.

What country are you from?

If you have an accent, this may seem like an innocent question, but keep in mind that it's illegal because it involves your national origin. Employers can't legally inquire about your nationality, but they can ask if you're authorized to work in a certain country.

Is English your first language?

It's not the employer's lawful right to know if a language is your first language or not.

In order to find out language proficiency, employers can ask you what other languages you read, speak or write fluently.

Do you have any outstanding debt?

Employers have to have permission before asking about your credit history and, like a criminal background history, they can't disqualify you from employment unless it directly affects your ability to perform the position you're interviewing for.

Similarly, they can't ask you how well you balance your personal finances.

Do you socially drink?

Employers cannot ask about your drinking, or even legal drug use, habits because these inquiries are protected under the American Disability Act.

For example, if you're a recovering alcoholic, treatment of alcoholism is protected under this act and if you don't have to disclose any disability information before landing an official job offer.

How long have you been working?

This question allows employers to guess your age which is unlawful. Similarly, they can't ask you what year you graduated from high school or college or even your birthday. However, they can ask you how long you've been working in a certain industry.

What religious holidays do you practice?

Employers may want to ask you this to see if your lifestyle interferes with work schedules, but this question reveals your religion and that's illegal.

They can ask you if you're available to work on Sundays.

LESSON 9

PERSONAL CREDIT
AND
UNDERSTANDING INSURANCE

Understanding Your Credit Score

Although most people realize their credit histories are chronicled in credit reports, 70% don't know they also have a credit score. And, this simple three-digit number may stand between you and a car loan or home mortgage.

The Early Show's financial advisor Ray Martin explains what these credit scores mean and offers tips on how to improve them.

You may ask, "If I know what's on my credit report, why do I need to know my credit score?" The answer is easy. Martin says, "Over 75% of mortgage lenders and 80% of the largest financial institutions use FICO scores in their evaluation and approvals process for credit applications."

While credit reports are a laundry list of your credit accounts, payment history and other information, your credit score—typically called a FICO score, named after the company that developed it, Fair Isaac & Company—is one number between 300 and 850. The higher your number, the better the chance you will make your loan payments and make them on time, lenders believe. It's much easier for lenders to look at this number than cull through our credit reports to come up with their own risk evaluation.

Although banks and other financial institutions have been using FICO scores for years, only in the past two years has the individual been allowed to learn his score. FICO resisted releasing scores for some time, afraid that consumers would use the data to artificially inflate their scores and thus make them less useful. However, pressure from Congress and consumer groups has changed that. But to most people, the revelation that they even have a FICO score is still news. To clarify, other companies can provide you with their own versions of a credit score. However, FICO scores are above and beyond the most-used score. FICO is so big that it's used interchangeably with the term "credit score." Most people call credit scores a FICO score. Other companies' numbers can give you a sense of how your credit is viewed by lenders, but if you really want to know how lenders see you, you need to check your FICO score.

What's in a score?

About 60% of people have credit scores of 700 and above. The best number to have is 720 or above. If your score is 720, there's really no need to try and raise it because lenders lump you in the same category as folks with a score of say 800 or 820. At 720, you are viewed as a safe risk and typically receive a loan without problem and at a low interest rate. However, if your number is below 700, it's definitely worth your time to try and pump it up.

Here is how Martin explains a FICO score is determined:

- ❖ 35% Payment History: "Having a long history of making payments on time and no missed payments on all credit accounts is one of the most important items lenders look for."
- ❖ 30% Amount Owed: "This measures the amount you owe relative to the total amount of credit available. Someone closer to maxing out all their credit limits is deemed to be a higher risk of late payments in the future and this can lower their credit score."
- ❖ 15% Length of Credit History: "In general, a credit report containing a list of accounts opened for a long time will help your credit score. The score considers your oldest account and the average age of all accounts."
- ❖ 10% New Credit: "Opening several new credit accounts in a short period of time can lower your credit score. Also multiple credit report inquiries can represent a greater risk, but this does NOT include any requests made by you, an employer or by a lender who does so when sending you an unsolicited, 'pre-approved' credit offer. Also, to compensate for rate shopping, the score counts multiple inquiries in any 14-day period as just one inquiry."
- ❖ 10% Types of Credit in Use: "Your mix of credit cards, retail accounts, finance company loans and mortgage loans is considered."

How to get your FICO score:

The website myfico.com will sell you a comparison of your three credit reports from the three main companies: Experian, Equifax and TransUnion along with your FICO score for $40. For this price you also gain access to a feature on the site that lets you create hypothetical situations, such as paying off a particular debt or paying credit card bills on time, etc., and see how such actions will affect your score.

Just like your credit reports, you have to buy your FICO score. Martin recommends buying a combo of the information. Because the score is compiled from your credit reports, you need to make sure all three are correct. Also, this format organizes credit information from each company side by side so it's easy to read.

You can buy credit reports separately from each company. The company will also provide you with a credit score. However, it won't be your FICO score, which is what you really need to know.

Boosting credit scores:

Although you can't raise your score overnight, you can do so fairly quickly. The scoring formula gives more weight to recent activity. So, even six months of "good behavior" will have an impact, demonstrating that you have cleaned up your act. Because payment history comprises the largest part of your FICO score, making a habit of paying bills and other payments on time is obviously going to have the largest positive impact. However, the fastest way to improve your score is to pay down balances. This lowers the amount of credit you're using relative to how much credit you have available to you. Remember, FICO scores reward people who use a smaller percentage of their available credit. Some people suggest never using more than 50% of your limit on any card.

Avoid opening a lot of new accounts at once—this makes lenders queasy—particularly if you don't have a long credit history. Many recommend not having more than five credit cards. If you decide to close some credit accounts, close the newer accounts first. However, don't close more accounts than necessary because this lowers your ratio of debt to available credit. Rotate and use all of your cards—a dormant credit account will not help your score. If you do have a late payment, it's worth a call to the lender to see if they will remove this information from your records in a "goodwill adjustment." You can choose to dispute the late payment report. While it's in dispute, the item will stay on your credit report but not factor into your FICO score. While there's no question that having a good credit score is essential, it's also important to point out that FICO scores do not take your age, income, assets or employment history into account. Specific lenders may pay closer attention to income, assets and employment history. Also, FICO scores treat all late payments equally. However, an auto finance company, for instance, can look at customized scores tailored for their industry. If you've been late on credit card payments but never missed a car payment, they may take this into consideration.

FICO (Most Common)		VantageScore	
Payment history	35%	Payment history	32%
Length of credit history	15%	Utilization	23%
Amounts owed	30%	Balances	15%
Types of credit uses	10%	Depth of credit	13%
New credit	10%	Recent credit	10%
		Available credit	7%
Total	**100%**	**Total**	**100%**

As you see the VantageScore formula uses 6 components, versus the FICO formula which consists of 5. What you need to keep in mind though is that each major component consists of several sub-components (of which the percentages for each aren't publicly available).

According to FICO's website, the "Amount owed" category consists of:
- ❖ Number of accounts with balances
- ❖ Amount owed on accounts
- ❖ Amount owed on specific account types
- ❖ Proportion of credit lines used
- ❖ Proportion of installment debt which is owed
- ❖ Lack of a specific type of balance, in some cases

Those 6 sub-components, when combines, equal 30% of your credit score. On the other hand, VantageScore doesn't have an "Amounts owed" category, but from their category names one can make an educated guess that they still look at those 6 sub-components. The difference is that it appears they aren't all grouped under the same mother category.

Are they apples to apples?

Obviously the credit score range is not the same on each but aside from that, is there a formula to convert them for an apples to apples comparison? Unfortunately not, since the formulas inevitably do differ slightly. With that said, you can use this rough approximation to estimate your FICO score based on your VantageScore (which is what most credit scoring websites will provide).

The bottom line?

We all want the best, but the highest possible credit score—the 850 for FICO—is almost unattainable. In fact, there are many loan officers that have been in the business for years who say they've never seen a perfect 850 before. Furthermore, you can have a credit score in the high 700's and it will usually get you the best rates. Ultimately, instead of focusing on reaching the highest credit score possible, concentrate your efforts on having:

- ❖ A good mix of credit (revolving accounts like credit cards as well as installment accounts, like mortgages, student loans, or car loans)
- ❖ Keep your credit utilization on revolving accounts low (no more than 30% of your limit, but ideally under 10%)
- ❖ The older the accounts, the better! If you have an old credit card you hate, don't cancel it. Keep it open and use it occasionally since that account may be helpful for your score given its age. However, if the card has an annual fee and you're not using it, then usually it does make sense to cancel.

Comprehensive Credit Repair

When researching this material, I realized there was not only a great amount of information to cover, but that this information would change frequently. By beginning with a Question & Answer format, it became possible to cover a lot of important material in an extremely concise way. We picked the most often asked questions and cross referenced them with sections of the book that go into more detail. The questions act as a sort of index to the entire book. If you find one that pertains to you, you can then go to the section that more fully covers that topic and get what you need. You can start here or skip ahead to the next topic.

Common Questions and Answers

Over the last 5 years, these are the most frequently asked questions that I have come up against. For many of students, finally getting a direction, even knowing that there is one, has been a great relief. I believe these questions and answers will do exactly that for you.

How Can I Pay My Bills For Only 5-10% of What I Owe Without Bankruptcy?

The thing most feared by creditors is that you actually will go bankrupt. In fact, even with the new bankruptcy laws, they still stand to lose everything you owe. By failing to pay your debt for a period of more than 6 months, you account will be written off as a loss. This is known as a "profit and loss write-off" or a "charge-off" which means the debt can't be collected. In fact, standard accounting practices dictate that any debt unpaid for 6 or more months must be considered uncollectible. At this point the debt is either sold or transferred to a collection or legal department.

Now that your debt is considered uncollectible, you can contact your creditors and offer to make a settlement. Most worry that if they don't accept something, they won't get anything, and are quite open to making a payment arrangement. They may ask you for an accounting of your finances to back up your contention that you can't pay them more than 5 or 10 percent of the debt (or 40% or whatever). You're not obligated to comply, but some sort of written response may speed their accepting your terms. Mind you, this is not a guaranteed system, but it is quite common to make settlements such as we describe here.

What Fill-In-The-Blank Letter Can You Use To Clean Up Your Debts And Credit?

Following the above strategy, we have included some forms with blanks for you to write account numbers and the amount of your settlement offers. These are also geared to protecting your efforts by clearly spelling out the terms of your new payment agreement.

How Do You Get Your Credit Report for Free?

There are a number of ways to do this, and some vary by state. One way is challenging an error on your report. The bureaus will generally respond with a copy of your report.

How Do You Make Your Debts Disappear?

There are two ways. The first is to wait. Unless your creditor has a court judgment against you on any particular debt, all record of the debt will disappear from your credit report in 7 years except for bankruptcy which lasts for 10 years. By simply waiting, time will erase your problem, and by opening up new accounts, you will get new credit, and a good rating. The second way is to pay off faster. By strategically refinancing your mortgage, you can use your equity to immediately pay off al the high interest credit you now have. Students of ours typically save as much as $1000 per month by using equity to kill off high interest debt. Then, by applying this savings to your principal, your mortgage will be paid at double or triple speed. This will save you literally hundreds of thousands of dollars.

How Can I Quickly Recover From Bankruptcy?

There was a time when bankruptcy stained your credit for decades. Not any more. An entire industry has sprung up to offer new credit to the recently bankrupt. Even mortgage companies will work with you, some when you begin your bankruptcy plan, and others after you've completed it, and/or waited 1 year.

How Can You Get a Credit Card When You've Been Declined Over And Over Again?

There are large numbers of 'secured credit card' programs for those who have been repeatedly declined credit. In this 'secured' arrangement, you establish a regular savings account with a bank offering such a card, say for $200. The bank then issues you a credit card with a $200 to $300 spending limit. Some banks use the criteria that your credit must be clean for the last three months. Others have absolutely no rules other than that you must put at least $100 in your new savings account.

Be advised that any money in your savings account is meant only as a hedge against your potential failure to pay. It is up to you to pay the bill each month. If you pay your bill on time, you can get unsecured credit in as little as six months and more every six months. In fact many secured card companies will give you an 'unsecured' or regular credit card with as much as a $2000 spending limit. This process of moving from secured to unsecured credit is an excellent and increasingly common way to establish personal history in the credit market.

How Can You Use Legal Pressure To Fix Your Credit?

Credit bureau reporting is controlled by an extremely strict set of laws and court rulings. One ruling in particular found that a credit bureau wasn't protected by the first amendment in the way a magazine or news gathering agency might be. The law says that so long as a publisher's error wasn't on purpose, they are 'held harmless'. The credit bureau, on the other hand, was ruled to be selling an information product which is purported to be accurate. When the product fails, whether by mistake or not, the bureau is liable for the damages they've caused, with no limitation. It's a product liability issue.

Bad credit can be repaired by identifying the errors in your credit, and bringing those to the attention of the credit bureau. Often, the will respond in the first round that they have inquired of your creditor and confirmed that the negative credit item is true. Even if that isn't so—they won't remove it. This is where you get out the bigger guns and inform them that they are obligated to have a "preponderance of systems in place" (see the Fair Credit Reporting Act) in order to avoid such errors. Merely reconfirming the initial error isn't good enough. If they refuse to do their job, you have still bigger guns yet. You file a formal complaint with the FTC.

How Can You Stop Your Creditor's Collection Efforts Cold?

You write your creditor a letter, certified—return receipt requested, stating that you will no longer honor their collection attempts, and that they may no longer contact you either by phone or in writing regarding your delinquent account. The Fair Debt Collection Practices Act tells us that the creditor can only call one more time, and then, only to tell you what they might or will do now that you have asked them to stop.

Can Asking About A Car Loan Trigger A Negative On Your Credit Report?

When you apply for a loan, an Inquiry is recorded on your credit. Too many of these can lower your credit rating. A creditor has the right to look at your credit if they have a reasonable belief that you might enter into an agreement involving the extension of credit terms. By writing to your credit bureau and explaining that you were shopping around, and did not say that you wanted credit, but merely pricing, you can get the inquiry removed. Today's scoring system better takes into account this 'shopping around' process. If you look at credit terms for a car over a two week period, no matter how many times, it will only show up as one inquiry.

How Can You Get The Lowest Interest On A Credit Card, Almost Like Getting An Interest Free Loan?

Many credit card companies offer 0% teaser offers for the first 6 months that you have the card. By switching your balance from one card to another, and moving from 0% offer to offer, you can borrow money at no interest almost indefinitely. However, record keeping is a vital part of this process.

Can You Get An Interest Refund Even If You Aren't Necessarily Owed One?

The rate charged by your credit card is open to a great amount of competition. If you call your creditor and ask that your rate be lowered somewhat, and include that you want the new lower rate applied retroactively, you can pay less now and get money taken off your existing debt. There is a fight going on for your business greater than at any time. Take advantage of competition.

Can You Turn Your Credit Debt Into Cold Hard Cash?

Under the Fair Debt Collection Practices Act, every violation costs the collection agency $1000 in fines payable to you. For example, your request that you are no longer contacted, if violated will net you $1000 in court. Many attorneys make their entire living exercising this law. By carefully recording your request that you be left alone and also recording phone calls from creditors using the record device on your answering machine, you will likely catch more than one creditor violating the debt collection laws. Some of our clients have turned a few hundred dollars in unpaid credit card bills into thousands of dollars in fines.

What Is The Chance I Will Be A Victim Of Identity Theft?

One out of five Americans will be victimized by this theft this year. That's over 38 million individuals.

Has Someone Stolen Your Identity?

A quick look at your credit report will tell you if there are accounts under your name that aren't yours. Or if you feel you're the victim of ID theft and have some proof, you may request a free report. Some unrecognized account may be for a person who shares your name, but it's important to clear up ownership of any unrecognized account.

When Shouldn't You Pay Off Your Credit Card Balance?

If you are delinquent on your bills, the only leverage you have is the money you still owe. Before you actually settle your debt, negotiate an agreement with your creditor that includes how it will be reported on your credit report. Ask them to agree not to respond to any credit bureau inquiries about the account's status. This way, when you finally pay, your bad credit will be removable. You can challenge the credit bureaus saying that you "don't believe the creditor will confirm the negative information on the report". Since your creditor has agreed not to as part of your payment terms, the item will be removed. The law states that any disputed credit unanswered within thirty days must be removed.

What Credit Card Industry Dirty Secret Can Cost You Big Time on Your Next Mortgage?

There is a policy found in the small print on many credit card applications that says essentially "no matter what rate we give you, if we find out in the future that you are late, or were late with another creditor, we can as much as double your rate." Suddenly, your manageable bills can become unmanageable and even one late mark on an account turns it from a good account into a bad one. This can suddenly change the income ratios used to judge your mortgage application. Remember; first and foremost; always pay your mortgage on time. This can mean a difference in all future debt negotiations.

Secrets Revealed

Who is the only person worth complaining to at a credit card company? TRAP—Financial companies are set up to block your efforts at changing policy. Everyone is allowed to say no. Few are allowed to say yes, especially early.

What are The 6 P's Of Successful Personal Finance Management?

Proper preparation prevents poor personal performance. Every part of this book is arranged to help you prepare and stay prepared. On our site, we offer free tools that can give you great advantages in preparing your numbers. For example, you can find out how to save hundreds of thousands of dollars by prepaying your mortgage. Any given extra payment each month will affect the overall outcome. Want to save embarrassment while shopping for a new car or home? Find out exactly what you can afford. Knowledge is power. After you have exhausted your efforts with customer service, the only place you will likely get satisfaction is with the legal department, or sometimes the recovery department, and occasionally the collections department. By complaining about specific violations of the Fair Debt Collection Practices Act, you will certainly get their attention. Always ask to speak to a manager, and become deaf to the word 'no'.

Organizing Your Credit Picture

Setting Your Goals.

Among the most important tools you can use in the pursuit of credit and financial success are planning and goal setting. So, where do you start? Set your goals and decide what corrective actions you need to take first. It may be that you need to correct poor credit. Maybe you need to consider bankruptcy or, having recently emerged from it, need a path back to the top. If you don't yet have a plan, this is the right place for you to start.

For those who don't immediately know which issue is in need of resolution, it is best to make a list of all your financial challenges. For some of you, it will be debt. For others, it might be income—you would like to earn more to reach your dreams—still others might feel that they simply need a plan where none exists now. Prioritizing your life is an ongoing challenge. Even for those with experience at following a self organized agenda, redoing this effort on a regular, at least annual, basis can be an enlightening exercise. Organizing involves writing, because without a written plan, what you hope for is likely to remain a dream, never to become fruitful reality. This is a time for making lists, for being honest and forthright with yourself.

Getting Organized.

Listing your debts is likely the most important first step in creating an overall plan. Once your debt has been mastered, you can then decipher the financial power available from your present income. From there, you can begin to decide what you need and what you will have to do to get it.

What is it about the necessary reality of facing debt that causes so many people to put their heads in the sand? Problems are rarely as bad as fearing them. When you understand exactly what you owe, you can figure out what you need to resolve that issue. Money is a tool toward fulfilling your goals. Planning, with an accurate view of your debts, is the way to reach those goals. Distinguishing amongst wants, needs, and desires is an additional important benefit of this exercise.

Looking at the Whole Picture.

We have added a worksheet that covers total debts, your monthly payments, and the interest rate associated with each, and we've also added the 'people' side of the equation. You will list who you have already spoken to in connection with a debt, whether or not more than one party (such as a collection agency) is involved, the type of debt, and how important that debt is to the overall picture.

Credit Reports . . .
Obtaining, Reading, Types Of . . .

How to Get Your Credit Report

In order to negotiate or fix your credit, you will need to see how it is reported. Experian (was TRW), Trans Union, and Equifax are the three largest companies that gather and resell credit information. It is necessary to obtain your credit history from each bureau to get a full picture, because any single reporting agency may or may not have a complete record of your activities. There is more than one type of credit report, and it is necessary to differentiate between them. The most common consumer version often fails to give credit score information—the main criteria for deciding what interest rate you will pay on a loan. A professional report obtained from a single credit bureau is referred to in the banking trade as an infile. It includes a credit score and a detailed record of how you actually paid your debts on a month-by-month basis. A report that combines at least two and preferably three individual credit bureau infiles is referred to in the reporting trade as a Trimerge, and in the mortgage trade as a full factual or residential mortgage credit report. This is a complete picture of your credit history used in making decisions for home and auto loans and other large purchases.

Steps To Get Your Report

You can get a free report from any credit bureau if it reported data used in a decision used to deny you credit. To obtain this free report you must submit the following information:

- ❖ A copy of the rejection letter of the creditor
- ❖ Your full name
- ❖ A copy of a photo ID
- ❖ Current address and previous address if different in the last 5 years
- ❖ A copy of your driver's license, social security card or a bill sent to your home address.

Credit bureaus provide a free report as part of a dispute resolution process, though Experian has been known to send an updated version of only the exact portion of your report in dispute. The three bureaus often have overlapping information, but just as often, they have disagreeing or unique entries on your credit history. It takes at least two reports to get a complete picture. Look at a Trimerge every six months and no less than 30 days prior to a major purchase. It costs approximately $8 to obtain a report from any of the three bureaus. You can find out the exact fee using the 800 numbers listed below. It may take up to thirty days to receive a response to your request, so be patient.

Credit Bureau Contact Information

Experian www.experian,com

(888) 397-3742
Or, for applicable states, to request your free report call (866) 200-6020.
Experian
P.O. Box 2104
Allen, TX 75013

Trans Union www.transunion.com.

(800) 916-8800
Trans Union
760 Sproul Road
Box 403
Springfield, PA 19064

Equifax Information Service www.equifax.com.

(800) 685-1111
Equifax Credit Information Services, Inc.
P.O. Box 740241
Atlanta, GA 30374

Credit bureaus change their addresses in an effort to thwart credit repair organizations, which are recognized by their use of old addresses in high volume dispute mailings. It is always a good idea to confirm the address by calling first.

Protect Yourself:

When sending correspondence, always do the following:

- ❖ Use return receipt requested/certified mail at the post office. This ensures that you have proof the correspondence was received.
- ❖ Photocopy everything you mail.
- ❖ Keep a file and document the date you mailed any letter.
- ❖ Send a second request if a response doesn't arrive within one month from the original letter date, sooner if it's urgent.

If you encounter delaying tactics when trying to get a report, it is often helpful to explain that you will contact the FTC to inform them of the credit bureau's failure. Credit bureaus are obligated by law to provide consumers with requested information within 45 days from receipt of a demand. Beware of tactics that include asking for documents that were already included and asking for additional proof of identity. If your address has changed often over the years, you may be denied a copy of your report because you are requesting it be sent to the 'wrong address'. Providing proof that you have received official bills or mail in your name at an address will cure the problem. In order to avoid these hassles, make your requests brief, your identity confirmation and photocopies clear, and your address consistent across all documents you provide.

How to Read Your Credit Report

Credit reports were originally intended for use by professionals, and are generally difficult to understand. More people have access to their reports these days, so the bureaus have felt the need, reluctantly, to make them somewhat easier to read. It is still difficult to fully understand all the coding and information gaps. Even some professionals are confused as to the meaning of the parts of a given report. Making decoding difficult is absolutely done with purpose. You can't fight what you don't understand.

Probably just as important to understanding how to read your report is figuring out how to fight what's wrong. Some bureaus, for instance, use a code of 1s and 2s to express if an account was paid on time or 30 days late. The trouble is a 1 can mean 30 days late on one bureau's report, or it can mean on time on another's; a 2 can mean either 30 or 60 days late, again depending on where you get your information.

Most accounts are represented by the following information:

* ❖ The name of the creditor and the type of creditor
* ❖ Your account number
* ❖ The status of the account—open, closed, past due . . .
* ❖ Whether individual payments were timely or late

A brief explanation of number and letter codes may be located on the back side of a consumer credit report. In some cases, credit bureaus will offer, for a fee, a more concise booklet on reading credit. This is self published as both a profit center, and a way of warding off complainers. ("Why don't you just buy the book, Sir?") Do not count on the bureau to provide you with advice on challenging reported information. Who owns the 'free credit' report sites? The credit bureaus own them. For a fee, after you have fallen for a marketing pitch, you will learn how to actually understand your credit.

Publications from banks, credit card companies, even the FTC traditionally say that it isn't possible to change credit reporting through credit repair. They suggest you wait for seven years for removal of bad credit. The major bureaus also provide useless 'explain yourself' areas to limit credit disputes. These offer you the 'right' to add your side of the story in up to 100 words. The problem is, credit is a numbers game and written excuses don't change the numbers. Explanations do nothing to resolve problem accounts or lower the higher interest you pay because of negative account histories.

Types of Credit Reports

Infiles

Although all credit reports start with the same basic data, they do not contain the same level of information. When you apply for credit, your potential lender sees an infile, as professional bureau reports are known. It contains much more information than a sanitized consumer report. This is especially true for the negative information. One feature of an infile often omitted from the consumer version is a national credit risk score known as a FICO score. It ranges from a low of 375 to a high of 850. Useful credit is anything above 720, although you can work with scores in the high 500's—at higher interest rates. Another piece of information on an infile is the lettered or numbered additions that appear under the score. These indicate exactly what factors have contributed to your credit score deficiency. Not surprisingly, they are called factors. You might see letter codes like a, d, e, m, s, b, or number codes like 34, 19, and 27. Some examples of factors are: too many accounts with open balance, too many delinquent accounts, proportion of balance to credit limit too high. The FICO score and the factors are perhaps the most informative infile components not found on most consumer versions.

Full Factual/Residential Mortgage Credit Reports

When applying for a mortgage, a report known as a full factual report is used to determine the outcome of your application. It is a combination of at least two of the bureaus' infile reports. It may also contain information about your lifestyle, such as:

- ❖ Employment and income
- ❖ Residence
- ❖ Details of your credit application

This information is verified by someone working for the bureau or agency compiling the report.

Reading Consumer Disclosures and Infiles

Account status and payment history are the two more important aspects of any credit report entry. Following is an overview of how to read this information from each of the three bureaus' reports:

Experian's Consumer Disclosure

Experian's consumer report emphasizes a few facts:

- ❖ You are responsible for your account.
- ❖ There is an amount of money you owe, and
- ❖ Whether or not you have made late payments to your account, although it does not say when. This makes it difficult to attempt the repair or removal of poor credit marks. If you cannot pinpoint when you are accused of having been late, it is quite a challenge to dispute it.

Consumer Disclosure Example

"Account is current and all payments being made on time. 60 days late was reported during the account's history. Scheduled monthly payments: $75.00, last payment was reported to Experian: 10/2004. Account balance: $2,708.00 on 10/2004. Months previewed 76."

Experian's Infile

Located in the right-hand column of an infile report is the following information:

Cur-Was 90
nnncccccccc12
nncc1nnncccc

"Cur-Was 90" states that a current account was ninety days late at some point in the last seven years. Your payment history is the letter and number code (nnnccc . . . 12), the first n on the middle row stands for the status of the account 24 months ago and the last c standing for the most recently reported month. Nothing was due on the account in months with an 'n'. The letter 'c' means money was in fact owed and paid on time. If your account was one month late, a '1' appears. If you go another month with no payment, a '2' is used.

"Cur-Was 90" is an account status that reflects your payment history. Since the status covers the past seven years, it is possible that all of the letter codes could be a 'c', indicating payments were made on time for the last 24 months, but at some time between two and seven years ago, you were 90 days late. Almost all consumers are confused by the combination of codes representing the last two years' indicating on time payment, and the account status representing the last seven years that says you were late.

Trans Union

Consumer disclosures and infiles are similar. Payment history on reports appears like:

111112311111   1 = on time, 2 = 30 days late, 3 = 60 days late
1111X1111112
56 2 1 1   This means '56 months of history reported, '2' 30 day lates, '1' 60 and '1' 90 day late marks.

The past 24 months are reflected in the top two lines, containing numbers/letters. The first line is two years ago starting with the number '1' (on time). The most recently reported month is reflected by the final '2' indicating that you are 30 days late. These numbers don't refer to the same months as Experian's code system. A payment made on time, in this report, is indicated by the number 1; thirty days late is represented by a 2. The third line is a notation of the account status indicating this particular account has been reported for 56 months and there is one ninety-day late payment, one sixty-day late payment and two thirty-day late payments. Since a ninety day late payment is represented by a '4' on the top two lines, and none are visible, you may conclude that it happened more than two years ago.

Equifax Payment History and Account Status

Equifax has experimented with plain English reports of differing types over the years, with predictably sanitized results. Their account payment history does a fairly good job of relaying the information, with some confusing points noted.

>>>30(2) 60 (1) 90 (0) 8/04-R2<<<
This says the account has twice been thirty days late, once sixty days late and never ninety days late. This final notation—8/04-R2 explains that the date of the sixty day late payment was in August 2004.

Note: "R1" may represent both an on-time and thirty-day late account. As in other reports, it may be hard to pinpoint the date of all late payments. For those unschooled in credit, this can make it hard to challenge. Equifax might only provide a history for accounts with negative credit reporting.

Point Of Confusion

When a credit report contains information from all three major bureaus, a muddle of their reporting features can result. This 'Trimerge', or 3 report combination, is made strictly for professionals and is very complete. Usually, the date of any lateness and the changes in lateness over the entire seven year period is easily discerned, making disputes easier.

The information here covers all three credit bureaus and their reporting styles, yet there are many sub-forms of credit reporting. Depending on the end use, the information released by the three major bureaus is distilled, edited, and embellished as need requires.

Common reporting errors still shine through though. Often, account information is not updated or just plain inaccurate. Just as often, it belongs to someone else. The mixing of identities has been a problem in credit reporting from its inception. When you examine your report, take the time to compare your billing information with their information, and double check the amount owed. It has a sneaky way of becoming more than you thought, or more than you agreed to. Often, payments are not credited on reports, even if the lender has done so on a statement. For all the flaws in this system, it is the system. Whatever manages to remain on your report after you get through with your repair work represents you—or the electronic version of you. No matter how incorrect an item is, regardless of the proof you have that it is wrong, it is the 'truth' until changed on the report. Only you can make sure what they report fits the facts.

Negotiations—Q&A

Beginning Your Negotiations

Debt negotiation has high stakes. The financial well being of you and your family hangs in the balance. More often than not your perseverance will count for much more than any clever turn of phrase, or quick witted counter offer.

Q & A

"I'm calling to make an arrangement to start paying on my account. The account number is _____. What is my current balance?"

If applicable you should ask: "What was my balance at the time of my default?" (If it's lower, you may be able to revert to it.) Finally, ask: "What are the minimum payments you will accept?" Your creditor will ask why you need a payment plan if you have never been in default, especially if you've been mostly on time to this point. If you are already delinquent, they may try for a lump sum payment. It is their job to get the most money quickly. They may offer you a payment plan that doesn't fit your budget. It is up to you to insist on a plan that can work, and will fit your income and debt level. In the end, they really only have the choice of accepting what you can and will pay.

"If I can't make the minimum payment, what do we do?"

No matter what you hear at this point, stick to your guns and insist on getting a payment plan that fits your needs. If the person you are talking to won't make a deal, ask for someone who can. At the first level of customer service, personnel usually have no power to do anything other than enforce the original agreement. Once you have someone who can make a deal, insist on a payment plan that fits reality. Agreeing to anything else might cause you to look at bankruptcy as an option—say so. Also say that you have other accounts that have agreed to cooperate and you need this creditor to be part of the entire picture or your plan may fail and no one will get paid.

"Will you freeze further interest, and deal with the original debt, not the one that it has grown into?"

Often, a creditor will forgo interest payments and focus on getting the principal. This is especially true with retail debts, where a large profit was already made on your purchase. Credit card firms who have collected high interest payments and are fearful of mounting defaults will also entertain freezing interest, either from the day you start negotiating or from the month of your default.

"How will my credit be reported now that I'm paying? Will you 'un-rate' my account?"

Unrated credit means that when you challenge the credit bureau to confirm the information reported, the creditor either doesn't answer, in which case the item is removed, or they answer that they don't have information on that account. Either way, they can't rate the account without proper information. You need to lock down exactly how paying your creditor will affect your past and future credit rating as part of any negotiated plan. Generally, if you pay 100 percent of your debt you can get an agreement that the creditor will stop reporting on your account, allowing it to become unrated. Though it is possible to get this 'unrated' debt settlement for less than 100 percent, creditors are understandably reluctant to let you have good credit for a discounted settlement.

"What about re-aging my account?"

Re-aging an account simply means that your creditor, usually in exchange for a payment, will dispose of old payment history on the account and report only newer, on-time payments.

"Will the account be listed as a 'settlement' on my credit report, or will you agree to un-rate my account if I pay you as agreed?"

You need to be specific in written agreements. Be clear that the word 'settlement' is not acceptable as a term of your paying off the debt. You must keep any deal you make with the creditor. This is your second chance. If you default on a renegotiated settlement, all bets are off.

"Why won't you help with credit reporting? Haven't you done this for other consumers?"

They may tell you that changes in credit reporting, or agreeing not to report isn't possible. Everything is negotiable. Most creditors have agreed to unrated settlements in the past. Say that you know that unrated accounts are common; if the person you are talking with can't make one, ask them to refer you to someone who can. The odds are against them showing you these cards in your first negotiation. They often read from a prepared script and don't have the authority to make command decisions. Also, it reflects poorly on them to fail in their collection effort.

"Will this new agreement, when complete, be considered payment in full?"

Be clear when making an agreement over the phone. The term payment in full or paid in full must be agreed upon. Follow up and solidify your agreement in writing before you pay. Unscrupulous collectors agree to anything you ask to get your money, with no intention of keeping their end of the bargain. They credit your payment, take their commission, and nothing changes on your credit report.

Legal Alternatives

After you have exhausted negotiation alternatives, you may only be left with legal means to convince your creditors to settle. We shouldn't sue if you don't have cause, but you can voice (in writing) your feeling that laws may have been violated and action on your part may be taken. Section 1692f of the Fair Debt Collection Practice Act is titled Unfair Practices. You can skim this section to see if you have been subject to violation under this law. Section 1692k is entitled Civil Liability. Quoting the Title, Section, and Sub-section of these two laws, even in an amateurish letter, will make an aggressive collection agency wonder if you have evidence of their unfair practices, and could possibly collect a big monetary award under their civil liability exposure. Since these laws were drafted to protect individuals from the unfair balance of power between creditor and debtor, you'll find that much of what is written could apply to one of your credit problems.

Why Do I Have To Use Letters If I Reach An Agreement On The Phone?

Just because you reach an understanding with someone from your creditor's company doesn't mean that will translate to your credit report. Sometimes, commissioned collection personnel will outright lie to you, agreeing to whatever will get you to write the check. By the time you seek to enforce the agreement, you find that they did not have the power to make it, or worse, they aren't still with the company. With a certified letter, you have proof of the date your terms were received, and create a legal trail should future disagreement result.

Is The Agreement 'Legal' If I Don't Have Something Signed By The Other Side?

You can create what is known as a 'restrictively endorsed' payment. Your letter dictates the terms agreed to in the phone call, and adds that cashing of the enclosed check or money order means that those terms have been agreed to. Send this letter twenty days in advance your payment and make sure to send it to an actual named individual at that organization. Merely sending a blind letter will not enforce your rights because automated systems often open and deal with consumer correspondence. You will need to do the work of finding someone who will make an agreement and document that agreement with a letter prior to sending your money.

What Are Some Of The Terms I Should Negotiate For?

Most important is that the payment or sum of the payments made over the term of your new agreement will constitute Payment in Full. This is distinguished from a Settlement which is still a derogatory credit entry. Next is an agreement that the creditor will no longer answer questions about the account from credit bureaus. This will allow you to tell the bureau that your creditor is not confirming the negative information. Information remaining unconfirmed for more than thirty days must be removed—and that is successfully negotiated, permanent, legal, credit repair.

What Terms Are Most Likely To Be Accepted?

A single lump sum is the most likely way to get a discounted settlement that is called 'paid in full'. Remember, especially when you hear the phrase "it's not possible", that everything is negotiable. You can test their resolve by saying, "OK then, no deal. Call me when you are serious." You'll be surprised how many phone calls you get within a few hours or days capitulating to your terms.

How Do I Prove That They Received My Information?

Send your letter through Certified/Return Receipt Requested Mail so you have proof of who received it and when. The return receipt must be signed and dated in order to complete delivery. The receipt comes back through the mail, generally within a week.

Does It Matter If I Write Well, With Perfect Grammar And Spelling?

As long as you get your point across, and do it as described so it is legally enforceable, you will appear to be a potentially difficult customer who is best dealt with and accommodated. It also doesn't matter whether you type or handwrite if it's readable.

What Information Should Be On My Correspondence?

Your name, address, phone number, account number, the amount they are asking for, the amount you're willing to pay, and the terms on which payment will be rendered (a lump sum, 12 monthly payments, for example).

Points to Remember

You should always push for a paid in full. Your final goal in negotiating settlement can also be 'paid as agreed' or 'account closed—paid as agreed'. Anything other than these listings will have a negative effect on your credit report. Creditors make their profits by collecting from their customers, not by reporting negative credit information. Creditors realize this, and often will agree to allow the deletion of negative items upon settlement of the debt. Creditors won't try to ruin your credit rating as a personal vendetta. It's strictly business. If it pays to collect from you and restore your rating to perfect, they will do this. Talk to them about money, not principles or morals. An example is, "I know you would love to receive the $3000 I owe you, but it will not help my credit report if you can't change my rating to 'paid as agreed'. I'm better off paying it to other creditors who will agree in writing to change my credit rating."

Summary

The preceding questions are geared toward pushing your creditors to an agreement in exchange for money. If you have already made a settlement, the only leverage you have is your offer to pay in full. If you've already paid, you can use legal pressure based on the past wrongful actions of the creditor or collection agent. If they think they might lose money or have to spend more money, they will be more eager to settle. Lending institutions lose money all the time and write off their losses. Doing so is a last resort for everyone—it affects profitability and can ruin your credit. By modeling your negotiation on the questions above, you can make a settlement that fits your budget and gets your creditor paid, leaving you with intact credit in the bargain. If you don't get what you want with your first negotiation, stick to your guns. Remember, if you already have a number of late credit marks on your account, there is little more a creditor can do to ruin your credit. By holding out for your position, no matter how long it takes, you will likely get the settlement you desire.

Collections / Ceasing Collections

Collection Issues

If an account has been transferred to a collection agency outside of the original creditor's organization, then you will have two negative report entries for that one debt. By using the Cease Collections Letter you can shut down the collectors and cause the debt to be transferred back to the original creditor. However, sometimes that debt has been outright sold, and no return will ever happen. Where it is possible, insisting that you have issues directly concerning the original creditor (such as failure to bill correctly, at the right address, in the right amount, product failure) may spur the process on. You can then negotiate with the original creditor to agree on a payment, deletion of the collection account, and an updating of their records to paid account or the like.

Collection agencies will always agree more readily to delete the negative listing than banks or credit cards. Why? They can change their rating, but you are still stuck with the original creditor reporting you late. Who cares if you have a 'paid as agreed' collection account: no matter what the rating, every collection is a negative mark. You need to get the collection agency to agree to remove their listing entirely from your report and have the original creditor change the rating to 'paid as agreed'. At the very minimum, you are within your legal rights to demand the removal of the collection account from your report. Some collection agencies will tell you they have no power over what the original creditor will do regarding your credit. To some extent, this is true. However, both the collection agency and the creditor want their money. If collected, the agency gets paid, and so does the creditor; therefore, it is to their advantage to cooperate. Explain that if they can get a written agreement from the creditor, you will pay them their money, or else you will find a better way to spend your cash. Collections often come from odd places. Doctor's bills that were supposed to be handled by insurance, parking tickets you never knew about, and the like can be very difficult to resolve. This is especially true when you deal with state or city government bureaucracies. Student loans are another dead end. These loans have enforced payment, and can be stripped from your tax refund. They have very little need to negotiate anything, never mind help your credit. Focus your efforts where headway is likely.

Points to Remember

In most credit organizations, there are many, many people with the authority to make settlements, accept pay agreements, and make changes on a credit report. Larger creditors, such as credit card companies or banks will require more pressure before they agree to delete a negative listing, but virtually every creditor will acquiesce with the right amount of pressure, persistence, and persuasion.

Ceasing Payments / Collection

If you've decided not to pay certain creditors, or to hold off on those who either won't settle at this time or want what you can't give, you can temporarily stop them from attempting to collect the debt while you deal with your first priorities. This is done by sending a cease collection letter. The legal, debt collection, or recovery departments are the areas of a lending organization most capable of making a deal with you.

If you have never paid late and have perfect credit (though unlikely if you are reading this), you should know that stalling your creditors with cease collections letters will add a number of derogatory marks to your credit report and may cause the lender to seek judgment against you. Carefully consider whether or not it is in your best interest to stop payment on or attempt to settle previously unblemished accounts.

The goal of the debt reorganization process is to fulfill an agreement in which you demand from your creditors that they report your account as unrated or paid in full in exchange for them getting their money back. If, after attempting to negotiate with creditors, you don't think you can restructure your debt, bankruptcy may be the only choice.

Judgment-Proofing Yourself

If you stop paying certain bills, you will eventually see legal papers demanding payment. You must deal with all legal correspondence, maybe hire a lawyer, and possibly even go to court to hold off default judgments. Withholding money as leverage to force a settlement can expose you to a judgment more often with mortgages and auto loans, though credit cards have also been known to sue if the debt is large. It is possible for the lender to gain a judgment against you within thirty days after you are mailed legal papers notifying you of your default and their intent to seek court relief. Your credit agreement and the law stipulate that they may seek a judgment after notifying you by mail, and giving you reasonable time to cure the default. If a lender does not send you a summons and complaint stating his intention to seek court relief, you aren't necessarily safe. More than a few creditors have snuck a case into court without proper service, believing (often correctly) that you won't have the wherewithal to fight them after the judgment is ordered.

Sample Cease and Desist Letter

DATE:

TO:

FROM:

REFERENCE:

Dear Company Representative,

❖ You are hereby notified under provisions of Public Laws 104-208, also know as the Fair Debt Collection Practices Act, that your services are no longer desired.

❖ You and your organization must CEASE & DESIST all attempts to collect the above debt. Failure to comply with this law will result in my immediately filing a complaint with the Federal Trade Commission and the Arizona Attorney General's Office. I will pursue all criminal and civil claims against you and your company.

❖ Let this letter also serve as your warning that I may utilize telephone-recording devices in order to document any telephone conversations that we may have in the future. Any future mail sent to me by your organization will be sent directly to the F.T.C. and AZ. Attorney General's Office for immediate prosecution!

❖ Furthermore, if any negative information is placed on my credit bureau reports by your agency after receipt of this notice, this will cause me to file suit against you and your organization, both personally and corporately, to seek any and all legal remedies available to me by law.

Since it is my policy neither to recognize nor deal with collection agencies, I will settle this account with the original creditor.

Sincerely,

Credit Bureau Dispute

Credit Bureau Dispute Letter

The following letter is used to dispute items directly with the credit bureaus when negotiation with your creditors won't work. This is especially true when the creditor is the government or the IRS, or if you're disputing public records.

Avoid the look of being coached. Customize this letter by altering the wording and layout. Even add a sentence or two explaining facts or details particular to your case. Remember, this letter is not based on a formula. It is a factual statement of your position and intentions regarding the creditor and an act of letting them know you believe they have made an error and that you are capable or pursuing it legally.

Use the creditor forms to record when you send this letter and the follow-up in thirty days. On subsequent letters include the phrase 'second notice'.

Remember to send this, and all creditor correspondence, by certified/return receipt mail. This will provide you with proof they have been notified, and show them you are organized and serious.

Note: After each account name and number you are disputing, you must include a specific reason why you think that credit entry is wrong. The reasons listed below are the more common ones, though you may list others. Do not, however, use an excuse such as, "I was late because I hurt my foot." The reasons that can cause a credit bureau to remove the bad credit must be rooted in the law, specifically, the Fair Credit Reporting Act.

Reasons why an account can be wrong:

- ❖ They didn't bill you correctly.
- ❖ They didn't send you a bill.
- ❖ This item is older than seven years (ten years for bankruptcies).
- ❖ This is not your account.
- ❖ You are not responsible for this account.
- ❖ You paid this account on time.

Sample Request for Dispute Resolution

To dispute information on your credit report, please complete this form and return it to Credit Reporting Agency.

Name:

Other Name(s):

Address:

Social Security Number:

Date of Birth:

Driver's License Number:

Telephone Number(s):

Fill out the information below. Check the reasons why you disagree with the information on your credit report.

Company Name:	
Account #:	
The Reason I disagree:	This is not my account I have never paid late This account is in bankruptcy This account is closed I have paid this account in full I paid this before it went to collection or before it was charged off
Other:	

Company Name:	
Account #:	
The Reason I disagree:	This is not my account I have never paid late This account is in bankruptcy This account is closed I have paid this account in full I paid this before it went to collection or before it was charged off
Other:	

Return this form to:

Signature:

(The dispute process is frequently done online)

Identity Theft

Beware: ID Theft

Identity theft occurs when someone uses your name, Social Security number, date of birth, or other identifying information to commit fraud. For example, someone may have committed ID theft by using your personal information to open a credit card account or get a loan in your name. For more information, visit www.consumer.gov/idtheft or write to: FTC, Consumer Response Center, Room 130-B, 600 Pennsylvania Avenue, N.W., Washington, DC 20580.

Has Someone Stolen My Identity?

A quick look at your credit report will tell you if there are accounts under your name that you didn't open. If you feel you're the victim of ID theft and have some proof, you may request a free credit report. An account you don't recognize may be for a person who shares your name, but it's important to clear up ownership of any unrecognized account.

How Do I Fight Identity Theft?

The Federal Government suggests the following steps when confronted by identity theft:

1. Contact the fraud departments of any of the major credit bureaus to place a fraud alert on your credit file. The alert requests creditors to contact you before opening any accounts or making changes to your existing accounts. As soon as the credit bureau confirms your alert, the other two credit bureaus will be automatically notified to place fraud alerts. Once the fraud alert is in place, you may request a free copy of your credit report from all three major credit bureaus.

2. Close the accounts that you know or believe have been tampered with or opened fraudulently. Use an ID Theft Affidavit when you are disputing new unauthorized accounts.

3. File a police report. Get a copy of the report to submit to your creditors and others that may require proof of the crime.

4. File your complaint with the FTC. The FTC maintains a database of ID theft cases that is used by law enforcement agencies for investigations. Filing a complaint also helps them learn more about ID theft and the problems of victims, so that more people can be helped in the future.

1. Fraud Alert

You have the right to ask that nationwide consumer reporting agencies place 'fraud alerts' in your file to let potential creditors and others know that you may be a victim of identity theft. A fraud alert can make it more difficult for someone to get credit in your name because it tells creditors to follow certain procedures to protect you. You may place a fraud alert in your file by calling just one of the three nationwide consumer reporting agencies. As soon as that agency processes your fraud alert, it will notify the other two, which then also much place fraud alerts in your file.

Equifax:	1-800-525-6285	www.equifax.com
Experian:	1-888-397-3742	www.experian.com
Trans Union:	1-800-680-7289	www.transunion.com

An initial fraud alert stays in your file for at least ninety days. An extended alert stays in your file for seven years. To place either of these alerts, a consumer reporting agency will require you to provide appropriate proof of your identity, which may include your Social Security Number. If you ask for an extended alert, you will have to provide an Identity Theft Report. An identity theft report includes a copy of a report you have filed with a federal, state, or local law enforcement agency, and additional information a consumer reporting agency may require you to submit.

2. Free Credit Report

You have the right to free copies of the information in your file ('file disclosure'). An initial fraud alert entitles you to a copy of all the information in your file at each of the three nationwide agencies, and an extended alert entitles you to two free file disclosures in a 12-month period following the placing of the alert. These additional disclosures may help you detect signs of fraud, for example, whether fraudulent accounts have been opened in your name or whether someone has reported a change in your address. Once a year, you also have the right to a free copy of the information in your file at any consumer reporting agency, if you believe it has inaccurate information due to fraud, such as identity theft. You also have the ability to obtain additional free file disclosures under other provisions of the FRCA. See www.ftc.gov/credit.

3. Debt Collectors Must Tell You the Facts

You have the right to obtain information from a debt collector. If you ask, a debt collector must provide you with information about the debt you believe was incurred in your name by an identity thief—like the name of the creditor and the amount of the debt.

4. You Can Block Credit File Information

If you belief information in your file results from identity theft, you have the right to ask that a consumer reporting agency block that information from your file. An identity thief may run up bills in your name and not pay them. Information about the unpaid bills may appear on your consumer report. Should you decide to ask a consumer reporting agency to block the reporting of this information, you must identity the information to be blocked, and provide the consumer reporting agency with proof of your identity and a copy of your identity theft report. The consumer reporting agency can refuse or cancel your request for a block if, for example, you don't provide the necessary documentation, or where the block results from an error or a material misrepresentation of fact made by you. If the agency declines or rescinds the block, it must notify you. Once a debt resulting from identity theft has been blocked, a person or business with notice of the block may not sell, transfer, or place the debt for collection.

5. You Can Stop Reporting of the Fraudulent Debt in Your Name

You may also prevent businesses from reporting information about you to consumer reporting agencies if you believe the information is a result of identity theft. To do so, you must send you request to the address specified by the business that reports the information to the consumer reporting agency. The business will expect you to identify what information you do no want reported and to provide an identity theft report.

To learn more about identity theft an how to deal with its consequences, visit www.consumer.gov/idtheft or write to the FTC. You may have additional rights under state law. For more information, contact your local consumer protection agency or your state attorney general. In addition to the new rights and procedures to help consumers deal with the effects of identity theft, the FCRA has many other important consumer protections.

How to Reverse the ID Theft

To successfully challenge the theft of your good name and credit should be easy, but it isn't. You need to go through a series of steps, including filling out an ID Theft Affidavit. This will make certain that you are, in the end, free of the debts and problems caused by the theft. Included is a complete form and format for fulfilling this task.

Instructions for Completing the ID Theft Affidavit

To make certain that you do not become responsible for any debts incurred by an identity thief, you must prove to each of the companies where accounts were opened or used in your name that you didn't create the debt. A group of credit grantors, consumer advocates, and attorneys at the Federal Trade Commission (FTC) developed an ID Theft Affidavit to make it easier for fraud victims to report information. While many companies accept this affidavit, others require that you submit more and different forms. Before you send the affidavit, contact each company to find out if they accept it. The affidavit has two parts:

Part One, the ID Theft Affidavit, is where you report information about yourself and the theft.

Part Two—the Fraudulent Account Statement—is where you describe the fraudulent account(s) opened in your name. Use a separate statement for each company you need to write to. When you send the affidavit to the companies, attach copies (NOT originals) of any supporting documents (for example, driver's license or police report). Before submitting your affidavit, review the disputed account(s) with family members or friends who may have information about the account(s) or access to them. Only information on accounts opened at the institution to which you are sending the packet.

Complete this affidavit as soon as possible. Many creditors ask that you send it within two weeks. Be as accurate and complete as possible. You may choose not to provide some of the information requested. However, incorrect or incomplete information will slow the process of investigating your claim. Print clearly. When you have finished completing the affidavit, mail a copy to each creditor, bank, or company that provided the thief with the unauthorized credit, goods, or services you describe. The companies will review your claim and send you a written response telling you the outcome of their investigation. Keep a copy of everything you submit.

If you are unable to complete the affidavit, someone with power of attorney may complete it for you. The information you provide will be used only by the company to process your affidavit, investigate the events you report, and help stop further fraud. If this affidavit is requested in a lawsuit, the company might have to provide it to the requesting party.

Completing this affidavit does not guarantee that the identity thief will be prosecuted or that the debt will be cleared.

DO NOT SEND AFFIDAVITS TO THE FTC OR ANY OTHER AGENCY

Remember:

1. If you haven't already done so, report the fraud passwords. Avoid using easily available information like your mother's maiden name, your birth date, digits of your Social Security Number or your phone number, or a series of consecutive numbers.

2. Any one of the nationwide consumer reporting companies can place a fraud alert on your credit report. Fraud alerts can help prevent an identity thief from opening any accounts in your name.

3. Contact your local police or the police in the community where the identity theft took place to file a report. The company you called is required to contact the other two, which will place an alert on their versions of your report, too. Get a copy of the police report or, at the very least, the incident report. It can help you deal with creditors who need proof of the crime. If the police are reluctant to take your report, ask to file a "Miscellaneous Incidents" report, or try another jurisdiction, like your state police.

4. You can also check with your state Attorney General's office to find out if state law requires the police to take reports for identity theft. Check the Blue Pages of your telephone directory for the phone number or check www.naag.org for a list of state Attorneys General. In addition to placing the fraud alert, the three consumer reporting agencies will send you free copies of your credit reports.

5. The Federal Trade Commission. By sharing (they will display only the last four digits of your Social Security Number) you will provide important information that can help law enforcement officials across the nation track down identity thieves.

   You can file a complaint online at www.consumer,gov/idtheft, or write to:

   Identity Theft Clearinghouse
   Federal Trade Commission
   600 Pennsylvania Avenue NW
   Washington, DC 20580

   Identity Theft Hotline
   1-877-ID THEFT

Send your correspondence and enclosures certified mail, return receipt requested.

Don't Live In Fear of Old Debt

What is old debt? It's a debt you thought was long since dead and buried that somehow rises to haunt you again.

Let's say that 10 years ago you ran into financial trouble. You couldn't pay one of your bills. The company tried its best to get the money. Eventually your account was turned over to a collection agency. It also tried its best but you just didn't have any money.

Eventually the credit card company faced reality and gave up on you. Your credit was seriously damaged for seven years.

A decade later you've turned things around. You pay your bills on time and your credit is now spotless.

Then one day you can get a call or a letter in the mail demanding payment for that bill from long ago. By now the penalties have driven the amount even higher. Fortunately, the collection company is willing to settle for less than half.

The company that contacted you is not the company that loaned you the money. It's a company that bought the debt, probably for just pennies on the dollar.

If you feel morally obligated to pay the debt you left behind then do it. But the reality is that you are no longer legally obligated to pay it.

Like all the other states Arizona has a statute of limitations on unpaid debts. With a few exceptions, most contract debts expire six years beyond the date from which the company could have sued you. For credit cards, it's three years.

Once that time has passed, the company can no longer legally chase you.

Don't misunderstand me: I think you should pay your bills. If you don't, then I think you should pay the consequences. But you have to pay the consequences only once.

Checking Account Issues

(Sample ChexSystems letter)

We regret we cannot open your account today due to information received from ChexSystems, Inc., a consumer-reporting agency. ChexSystems did not make the decision to disapprove your account application and is unable to provide you with specific reasons why the decision was made.

You have rights under state and federal laws. Included in these rights are:

❖ The right to obtain a free copy of your ChexSystems consumer report if you make such a request to ChexSystems within 60 days of your receipt of this notice; and

❖ The right to dispute the completeness or accuracy of any information contained in such report by notifying ChexSystems directly of your dispute.

You may contact ChexSystems by visiting their web site at www.chexhelp.com, by telephone using their Voice Response Unit at 800-428-9623, by mail at ChexSystems Inc., Attention Consumer Relations, 7805 Hudson Rd., Ste. 100, Woodbury, MN 55125, or by fax at 602-659-2197.

Insurance Overview

Insurance is a major expense that we will incur throughout our lives. You will, at the very least, have to look into purchasing most of the following types of insurance:

- ❖ Auto
- ❖ Health
- ❖ Life
- ❖ Home Owners
- ❖ Business Liability
- ❖ Legal

The expense of having insurance coverage versus the impact of needing it and not having it speaks for itself. Auto insurance is mandated by law in all states, and it is a very worthwhile thing to have. If you have an auto accident a single emergency room visit with an ambulance ride can cost up to $7500 or more and the repair costs of a simple fender bender can cost up to $5000 to fix at a discount auto body shop. These figures are 5 times what a years worth of insurance generally costs. Insurance is a great benefit, not a nuisance. Health insurance will be the most costly of the different types of coverage you will need. Many jobs start without health insurance coverage until a set period of "probationary" employment has been reached. Some of the most common health plans available today include individual major medical and indemnity policies offered by many different companies. Check with your local state insurance regulatory agency for a competitive comparison of companies and coverage. One Stop Centers and most DES offices in all states have information about most types insurance. Auto insurance rates and other types of insurance can be researched online by doing a keyword search for "auto insurance" or whatever type of insurance you are seeking. Do your homework and do not jump at the first deals that come your way. When setting a household budget be sure to include insurance, and be sure to keep the premiums (usually set up as monthly payments) paid on time. Just one accident can wipe out your hard earned savings, so always embrace your insurance coverage rather than regretting it. This lesson is meant to send you after the information and encourage you to use insurance as a tool for your success.

Tips:

- ❖ Most insurance companies are divided into two major categories—life/health and property/casualty. Use their websites to learn about the rates and types of plans available.

Using Legal Insurance to Reduce Your Risk of Recidivism

Recidivism among prison inmates releasing back into our communities is approximately 50%-85% nationally within three years of release. Over 90% of those re-offenders do so within their first year. For inmates under 25 years of age, the percentage of recidivism is over 90%. Simply offering incarcerated offenders programming, education, and treatment is not enough to impact this problem.

One factor in the recidivism rates is the X-Factor. The X-Factor is the "Ex-Offender Factor". Ex-offenders are far more likely to come into contact with law enforcement than a typical individual. When these encounters occur, the ex-offender is often treated differently than a non-offender. The benefit-of-the-doubt that a non-offender receives is typically absent in these encounters. There are also many situations that an ex-offender encounters that require special consideration. A few of these are housing issues related to "Crime Free Communities", employment issues related to business insurance and potential discrimination, and even simple automotive issues related to moving violations and accidents. When these legal situations occur, the use of legal insurance coverage becomes a critical factor in the potential outcome. Just having competent legal counsel at hand can affect a person's decision-making process in a positive way.

Most legal insurance coverage basic services offer a 24 hour/7 day toll-free contact with an attorney. The service allows someone to call a lawyer to consult with within a matter of seconds for any situation that occurs, or for strategic advice where the ex-offender status may create a potential future problem. In any case, getting legal advice and thinking about the legality of situations in advance creates a positive and proactive thinking process that will, in and of itself, greatly reduce potential recidivism. Legal insurance coverage has a monthly preset number of free legal consultations, legal letters, and discounts on legal representation from experienced attorneys. This type of service can provide ex-offenders with a greater feeling of safety and self confidence, and the average cost is about $1 per day.

By doing an internet search for "legal insurance" or "legal shield" you will find many articles and companies that provide this service. One such website is found by going to Legal Shield, Inc. via Google or any search engine online.

LESSON 10

PERSONAL FINANCES

SETTING BUDGETS

PAYING TAXES

Tips for Lesson:

❖ This lesson is very important. Some very useful materials are provided, but this is a lesson that must be taught in a proactive manner. Only by setting a positive and serious tone will this lesson succeed.

❖ "Living Within One's Means" is the key point to this lesson. You will have to obtain current tax forms for the students since these frequently change.

❖ A forum for inmates to track their own finances and other budget-related materials provided round out the lesson, but as with all sections, your own unique personal input, within policy guidelines, is the key to its success.

Dependability & Reliability

❖ **Dependability:** You will be on time and at work every day. You will notify your supervisor when you cannot be at work.

❖ **Reliability:** You will follow through with a job. You look for things to do after completing assigned tasks.

❖ **Dependability and Reliability**: Will only take you so far. Getting a GED and continuing to earn certificates, credits, or even a degree, will put you in a position to earn the kind of money that improves the quality of life.

❖ **Steady Employment**: This should be everybody's goal; but try to make time for education to carry you even further.

****

EDUCATION AND EARNINGS
(1998 Figures-Add 20% for 2007)
(U.S. Department of Labor)

Level of Education	Average Monthly $	Difference
No High School Diploma	$508	N/A
High School Diploma	$1080	105%
Vocational Certificate	$1303	21%
Some College—No Degree	$1375	27%
College Degree	$2339	117%
Advanced Degree	$3331	208%
Professional Degree	$5067	369%

Withholding Taxes in General

Federal Income Tax: 15% is a good low side average.
FICA (Social Security): 7.5% employee's contribution 15% Total
State Income Tax: 3% 20% of Federal Income Tax (Variable)

173 hours per month = Full Time or 40 hours per week.

$ Per Hr.	$ Per Month	W/H	Net Income	2 People
$ 6.00	$ 1038.00	20%	$ 830.40	$ 1660.80
$ 7.00	$ 1211.00	21%	$ 956.69	$ 1913.38
$ 8.00	$ 1384.00	22%	$ 1079.52	$ 2159.04
$ 9.00	$ 1557.0	23%	$ 1198.89	$ 2397.78
$ 10.00	$ 1730.0	24%	$ 1314.80	$ 2629.60
$ 11.00	$ 1903.0	25%	$ 1427.25	$ 2845.50
$ 12.00	$ 2076.00	26%	$ 1536.24	$ 3072.48
$ 13.00	$ 2249.0	27%	$ 1641.77	$ 3283.54
$ 14.00	$ 2422.0	28%	$ 1743.84	$ 3487.68
$ 15.00	$ 2595.0	29%	$ 1842.45	$ 3684.90

Est. Monthly needs for 1 person

Rent—shared/roommate $ 300.00

Food—@ $10 per day $ 300.00

Car—$5000—Car w/maint. $ 200.00

Gas—@ 20 mile per gallon $ 90.00

Insurance—Basic $ 100.00

Clothes—Minimum $ 100.00

Phone & Utilities—Minimum $ 100.00

Recreation @ $5 per day $ 150.00

Total $ 1340.00

Est. Monthly Needs for 2 people

Rent or House Payment $ 600.00

Food—@ $15 per day $ 450.00

Car—X 2 $ 400.00

Gas—X 2 $ 180.00

Insurance @ 1.75 $ 175.00

Clothes—X 2 $ 200.00

Phone & Utilities—@ 1.5 $ 150.00

Recreation @ $10 per day $ 300.00

Total $ 2455.00

Form W-4

The Payroll Department will use this information to determine the amount of Federal income tax to withhold from their gross earnings.

- ❖ The top portion of the front page is a worksheet for the employee.

- ❖ The bottom portion of the front page will be given to the employer.

- ❖ Your students need not be concerned with the back page of this form.

- ❖ I strongly recommend your students select Single with 0 Allowances, irrespective of their marital status and/or number of dependents.

- ❖ This will ensure that they have enough withheld to pay their tax, and there's a good chance they'll get a tax refund when they file.

Form I-9

- ❖ The Employer must inspect this information to verify that a person is authorized to work in the U.S. (this is for immigration purposes).

- ❖ Your students will be required to complete the front page, Section I.

- ❖ The employer must complete the remainder of this form for the I.NS.

- ❖ Your students should familiarize themselves with the information on the back page titled LIST OF ACCEPTABLE DOCUMENTS. They will have to provide the employer with their specific identification information.

Tips:

- ❖ I suggest using Forms W-4 / I-9 for the students to fill out as practice.

- ❖ I strongly recommend that your students omit their SS Number and birth date from their forms to prevent identity theft. They will provide this information to their employer at the appropriate time.

Spending Plan Guidelines

1. Rent or Mortgage Payment...20-35%
2. Mortgage Taxes and Insurance, Association Dues if not included above...
3. Home Maintenance, house repairs, garden needs, pool needs.................
4. Groceries, cleaning supplies, beverages, paper products 15-30%
5. Food Away from home, lunches, dining out...
6. Utilities, gas, light, water, phone, garbage, sewer.......................................4-7%
7. Insurance, Life, Auto, Health not payroll deducted ....
8. Car gas and oil, lube jobs, repairs, registration 10-30%
9. Other Transportation, Taxi, Bus, Car pool, Parking.................................
10. Education, tuition, books, special lessons ....
11. Monthly medical and prescriptions not listed as debts 2-8%
12. Clothing costs 3-10%
13. Laundry and dry cleaning...
14. Club and Union Dues not payroll deducted ....
15. Newspapers, magazines, books, tapes & CD's ....
16. Beauty—Barbershop, Nails...2-4%
17. Personal Expenses, tobacco, alcohol...2-4%
18. Contributions & Gifts, church donations, presents 2-4%
19. Recreation, movies, hobbies, sports, vacations, entertainment 3-6%
20. Other expenses, kids allowance, postage, cable TV, other services, pets ....
21. Alimony and/or Child Support payments not payroll deducted ....
22. Babysitting and Child Care Costs ....

Figures in the box above are suggested spending plan limits for each category. Variations are due to income levels, family size and primarily personal choice. Categories that do not have a percentage represented are determined as needed; no suggested limits since they vary greatly from person to person.

Inmate Financial Log

Month: _____

Year: _____

Starting Balance: $ _____

Ending Balance: $_____

Date	Starting Balance	Store Purchase (-)	Additional Purchases (-)	DOC Charges (-)	Unknown Charges (-)	Work Pay (+)	Mail Money (+)	Gate Fee (-)	Ending Balance

*Use this form to practice tracking your finances while you are here so you will continue to do so after your release.

☞ *Good habits start here.* ☜

The Only 2 Financial Rules
You Need Live By

There's a lot of advice out there for saving money. But if it overwhelms you, start with just these two simple rules and you'll be on your way to financial independence. When it comes to the way we think about money, I've noticed there are two kinds of people: those who think $1,000 is a lot of money, and those who think $10 is a lot of money. I fall into the second category, but I'm not especially frugal. I have a nice car, take a vacation every year, and it isn't too hard to convince me to drop a few hundred dollars on a great pair of shoes now and then. I've never even clipped a coupon. But I've also maxed out my retirement savings, bought a house, and live without debt—all on an average salary.

What I've done isn't extraordinary, but it does seem rare. That said, I think most people can accomplish this fairly easily. All you have to do is live and die by two simple rules . . .

1. Pay yourself first: The best kind of cliché

"Pay yourself first" is a very common piece of financial advice. It's simple enough to follow, but that doesn't make it easy. If you can save $200 per month at 6% interest, you'll have more than $200,000 in 30 years. At the very least, you'll have a great savings fund at the ready for whatever life may bring. But how can you come up with that cash hen you barely have any money left between paychecks?

The answer is to take that money off the top. And yes, it'll sting a bit at first.

I've made a habit of taking contributions to my retirement and savings accounts right off the top of each paycheck on the very day it hits my bank account. I try to cut pretty deep too, leaving myself just a little more than I need to pay expenses. This works on two levels: It forces me to really budget to meet my basic expenses while keeping extra cash out of easy reach. I can still retrieve the money from my savings account if I happened to need it, but because I have to make a decision to transfer funds, they usually just stay put. I allow myself to spend whatever I don't need for expenses on whatever I like—if I don't spend it by the time my next paycheck comes, I roll that into savings, too.

I also save any additional money I get. I think a raise, tax return, or bonus can go two ways. It can raise your standard of living, or it can raise your standards. Rather than creating more expenses to suck up these extra dollars, I live the same way day to day and tuck the extra money away for something better.

2. *Practice mindful spending*

Having some leeway in your paycheck isn't a given, but I think many people have more wiggle room than they realize. This is what I mean when I say that I think $10 is a lot of money. When I decide to buy something, it's a decision, not an impulse buy. I want to spend my money on things that really have value for me, not just things that are convenient or appealing at the moment. So while I can buy something nice once in a while—without guilt—I have a hard time going out for lunch or buying (you guessed it) a latte.

Less expensive purchases are an easy mental hurdle to get over because they're so small it seems that they could hardly amount to anything. Truth is, these seemingly insignificant purchases can easily amount to, or exceed, that $200 you are aiming to save.

If you spend $4 every morning on a latte, and $12 each work day for lunch, this adds up to $80 per week—for a grand total of $4,160 per year. If you earn $50,000 per year, that's a full month of your salary. Do you really want all that money to amount to a bunch of coffee and Subway sandwiches?

This isn't to say that no one should ever buy a latte. But if I spend this kind of money every week, I don't have anything to devote to my savings. That's a sign that these seemingly small indulgences just aren't affordable, at least for me. This is why I've also decided not to opt for cable TV or any expensive cell phone plan. I don't' feel that I live like a pauper. After all, I have money saved that I can turn to not only in an emergency, but also to pay for things that I feel really add enjoyment to my life, rather than just distracting me for a few hours or days—and steadily subtracting dollars from my bank account.

What are your rules?

Over time, I've learned to save money as diligently as I pay my bills; I also try to spend what's left as mindfully as I can. I can't say I always succeed, that I never overspend or that I'm not often tempted to break the rules.

Nevertheless, I'm sticking to the strategy that has kept me out of debt, and helped me save enough to meet some key financial goals—and still have some fun. I know of other people who've done even better by employing these rules much more stringently than I.

As for me, I'll keep saving up for my next big purchase by keeping the little ones in check.

10 Simple Habits to Help You Save

People often think it's hard to save money, but there are actually a lot of little things you can do to save cash that really aren't all that difficult. And as with any activity, once you start doing them on a regular basis, they can become commonplace—almost habitual.

Carrying Cash

Carrying cash is probably one of the most useful money saving habits. Having to tear each bill from your wallet has a much greater impact than just swiping a piece of plastic.

Shortchanging Yourself

This is a habit some credit card companies have picked up on that you can do with your cash purchases. When you go out and buy something, take the leftover change and put it in a jar, then round the amount of the purchase up to the next dollar on your budget. For example, say you buy something for $2.32. Take the change (68 cents) and put it in your change jar. Then round the amount of the purchase up to $3 in your budgeted expense line. It's kind of like double-dipping; not only do you save the change, but you deny yourself a future 68 cents in that budget category.

Debit or Credit?

It doesn't matter if you use debit or credit cards, if you always make sure there is money in your accounts to cover all purchases when the bill arrives or the money is deducted from the account. This way you never owe interest on your credit and you're never charged for overdraft fees. Paying a bank to utilize your money for what are regular transactions is a bad habit.

Paying Bills as Soon as they Arrive

With items like utility, credit card, insurance, medical, and similar bills, make sure you pay them as soon as you get them. This avoids late fees due to having forgotten or misplaced a bill.

Financial Tracking

Use several simple spreadsheets to track a variety of assets and asset trends. When you find a system that works and you like, use it regularly until it becomes habitual.

Expense Tracking

This allows you to know where your money goes, provides an understanding of how much of it you need, lets you know what you can do with the excess, and helps you to stretch your dollar.

Habitual tracking is only half the battle when it comes to keeping your money in line. By having an idea of where your money goes, you can regulate and watch the outflow by keeping a monthly budget. Break your expenditures down into categories such as housing, food, entertainment, office supplies, clothing, health, transportation, and miscellaneous.

Period-Over-Period Comparison

Every month, do month-over-month comparison. This gives you a better idea of what and where you've gained or lost from last month and provides a record that allows you to then gauge trends and do year-over-year comparison.

Statement Reviews

Mistakes can be made. Billing errors may be more common than you think, and this is why you must review and check what you've been billed and for how much.

Setting Financial Goals

Setting financial goals is probably your best money habit. Use the goal-setting lessons that you've learned in Lesson 2 and apply them to your financial goals.

The Secret to Living Well on $11,000 a Year

This is the experience of a New Jersey man and his simple lifestyle. Glenn Morrissette is a professional musician, able to work from any location on his computer.

Why did you decide to live in an RV?

I had an apartment in Burbank and was the typical Los Angeles apartment dweller. I started to feel a strong desire to simplify my life. I had a garage full of stuff I never used, my closets were full, and I started to see that it was costing me money to have an apartment big enough to hold all the stuff I never use.

My initial plan was to scale back and move into a smaller apartment. Before long, I realized I didn't need too much to be happy. I could fit into a small space. That's when the RV idea occurred to me. I was just sitting in traffic and an RV pulled up. I said, "I could probably fit in that thing." The more I looked into it, the more I realized how practical it would be. For what I was paying form rent in LA, I could own my "house" free and clear and not pay rent, and own my car as well.

How do you stay under $11,000 a year?

The two key things that make it possible are not having rent or a mortgage payment. I own my RV, so that was an initial expense of about $14,000, but I have no house or car payment. Gas is controllable; I don't' drive if I don't want to. Most months, I spend less than $300 on gas. I estimate that I save about $1,000 a month compared to what I was spending in LA.

What do you eat?

I eat pretty well. I don't skimp on food. I eat a lot of grass-fed meats, fruits, and vegetables . . . some people call it the caveman diet. I go to farms, farmers markets, and health food stores. I probably spend about $250 a month on food. I could spend a lot less if I didn't care about eating well.

Do you have health insurance?

Yes. I'm self-employed so I purchase my own plan. I have a high-deductible plan and pay $80 per month. It would be even cheaper if I was 28. I don't' understand young people who say, "I can't afford health insurance." Last year, my appendix ruptured, and the insurance was a life-saver. I learned my lesson.

What about clothes?

I'm a pretty basic jeans and T-shirt kind of guy. I don't have to go to the office, so I don't need a wardrobe. I have 9-10 shirts and a couple pairs of jeans. I do have a suit so I can get dolled up when I have to, but my normal wardrobe is pretty minimal. I do one load of laundry every week, and I don't see the point of owning more clothes that I can do in one load of laundry.

Do you spend money on entertainment?

I don't go out much at all. I prefer the food I make to what I get in restaurants. More often than not, I'm disappointed. I'm pretty health-conscious and I want my food to be real foods, so I'm content eating what I make. The idea of spending $30 at a restaurant—that seems like four to five days' worth of food to me. Years ago, I ate out every single meal. I'm kicking myself now; if only I had invested that money instead.

I'm not a big drinker, although I drink somewhat socially. I'm a pretty simple guy. Music is my life. Even if I'm not working, if I have a free day, I will spend a big chunk doing music. It's a profession and a hobby.

Do you splurge on anything?

The food I eat. I don't' feel like I'm skimping at all. It's a form of health insurance to me.

And I just try to put myself in interesting places. I'm surprised how easy it is to do that. A lot of stuff is free out there. There's a lot of beautiful scenery in this country and it doesn't cost anything just to park. You can just drive into a national forest and live there for two weeks. I always try to give myself great real estate, whether it's by an ocean, a lake, or in the center of a cool little town. So I always have a great front yard, real estate that people would pay millions of dollars for, and it doesn't cost me anything.

I'm pretty frugal otherwise, and I don't miss it. I used to be part of the whole consumerist cycle, buying stuff I didn't need, and I don't do that anymore. It's liberating. I can maximize my savings. That's true freedom, to get to the point where I can say no to work anytime I want because I have a big enough nest eff. I'm not there yet, but that's my goal.

Do you have a retirement account?

Yes. I'm an avid investor. I guard my nest egg like crowned jewels. But I don't' see myself ever retiring. I love what I do. I'd much rather do what I love and live small, and enjoy life.

The Secret to Living Well on $40,000 a Year

Danny Kofke, a father of two, claims his family of four can live well on his $40,000 a year salary. Excerpts from his book, <u>A Simple Book of Financial Wisdom</u> appear below.

It's pretty impressive that you have supported our family of four on less than $40,000 a year. How did you do it?

This took long-term planning. Raising a family of four on my teacher's salary would be next to impossible if we had a huge mortgage and a lot of debt. Before we had children, my wife, Tracy, was a teacher, too. We had a plan for her to be able to stay at home once we had children. We weren't exactly sure when this would happen (this is for The Man Upstairs to decide), but we had an idea on when we would start trying. We ended up being married four years before Ava was born. During this time, we tried to live off one of our teaching salaries and used the other one to pay off debt and establish an emergency fund. We were not sure how long Tracy would be able to stay home—we initially aimed for one year—but we were able to have her stay home for six years and work part-time for one. We were able to do this even after having our younger daughter, Ella, three years after Ava. The key for us was the long-term planning.

Can anyone really succeed at this?

I do feel that almost anyone can. I know there are some that earn a lot less than I do or have more debt but I feel they can work towards this, too. I am not a financial major of a chief executive of a company. I have never even taken a financial class in my life. If this 35-year-old schoolteacher can learn the basics of money management and finances, then others can, too.

Tell us some of your more unusual advice that we might not have heard before.

I think the biggest thing I have learned is if broke people are making fun of you and laughing at your ways, then you are doing something right. It was difficult to get mocked when Tracy was working and we choose to live off one salary while others were spending like there was not tomorrow. Many people told me to get off my wallet and spend money. Pride is sometimes a hard thing to swallow, but I knew that many of these people were not making smart financial decisions and these decisions would eventually come back and hurt them. I don't know if it is unusual advice, but when making financial decisions, you have to do what is right for you and not be influenced by the many temptations that surround us.

What's the hardest financial rule for you to follow personally?

Living below my means is the toughest rule for me to follow. There are so many temptations—Madison Avenue spends billions of dollars each year to get our money—and sometimes I want to buy things I know I should not. When this occurs, I allow myself a 240-oyr breather and, if I still feel strongly about buying that object after that time, I will discuss it with Tracy. The great thing is, after I let the emotional aspect have time to go away, my more rational side speaks to me and I make a sound decision.

How are you teaching your children about money?

Once my older daughter, Ava, turned three, we had her do simple household chores so we could teach her how to handle money. I am not a fan of rewarding others for things they should be doing anyway, but I did make an exception with Ava since my initial goal was to teach her money management skills.

We started with chores that were easy for her to complete: cleaning her room, brushing her teeth. Every night, we would check off the chores that were completed, and every Friday we added them up and she was paid. We called this money what most parents do: an allowance. No matter what you call it, make sure your child does the work to earn the month. After Ava got paid (she could earn up to $1 each week), she had three jars: Give Away, Savings, and Spending. She first put 10 cents in the Give Away jar, 25 cents in the Savings jar and the remaining amount in the Spending jar. This worked so well for us. When we were at the store, often Ava would see something she wanted. We never had any arguments; we would simply say, "We'll have to go home and see if you have enough money in your spending or savings jar to buy it."

Ava has used the money in her Give Away jar in numerous ways. One year there was a little girl at my school who lost her father shortly before Christmas. Ava used her Give Away money to buy this little girl a stuffed animal. Ava actually came to my school and delivered this to her personally. Another year, Ava used this money to buy canned food for needy families in our community. This past Christmas, there was a family at her school that was struggling. Ava used the money in her Give Away jar to buy them a gift card to a local grocery store.

If Ava continues to apply these lessons in life—gives away 10 percent of her money, then saves 25 percent of it and uses the remainder for spending—and goes above and beyond in her job, she will be wealthy in more ways than a fat bank account can show.

Investing Made Easy: An Ex-Offender's Guide to Saving for the Future
By Joseph L. Chiappetta, Jr.

For many leaving prison, the idea of starting investments and financial management might as well be like planning a trip to Mount Everest on the way to the parole office. The terms are difficult to comprehend, and the steps to take are debated, even among experts. Financial management is easier than you think and should be on the top of your daily to-do list instead of a far-off plan. The problem with investing is the marketing that prevails. Presented below are 5 basic principles of investing, and the value of saving money in your daily life. Much of this information is based on Paul Merriman's *Financial Fitness* lectures, the rest on my own research and experiences. Five dollars per day can start you on your way to success. Five dollars per day is approximately $1,850 dollars a year. This kind of investment can earn you $1,000,000 over 30 years of doing it. There are 5 basic principles to investing, but there is only one rigid rule . . . continually save money and deposit it in your own portfolio. Portfolio . . . now there's a word. This is simply where and how you divide and invest your saved money. It's that simple. If you keep it all in a savings account, that's your portfolio.

❖ **Principle #1: "Ask the right person for advice."**

There are 3 groups that are the primary sources of financial advice and information.

1. **Wall Street**. These are the large firms that employ hundreds of Ivy League College Graduates and spend millions in advertising to encourage you to give them your money to invest for you . . . for a fee. They are in business to make money from your investments, so they are probably the worst choice. They stay in business and continue to gain new customers because they do all the work for you. Some people prefer this to having the responsibility on their own shoulders.
2. **Main Street**. These are your friends, neighbors, co-workers and family. They tell you what they did with their investments and financial management that worked for them. They are only slightly better than the Wall Street firms; they may not be able to properly explain their success, or may have only been lucky, not skilled.
3. **University Street**. These are the Academics, the College Professors and Expert Consultants who accurately track the real world results of the financial markets and report these facts without "spinning" them for effect of for marketing purposes. They are the guardians of the facts and the history of how they occurred. They study the markets as a source of historical and empirical data, not to encourage or persuade others to invest their savings. *Because of this, they are the BEST source of investment information.*

❖ **Principle #2: "Choose the best place for your investment money."**

This is about choosing *Smart Diversification*. Smart Diversification is dividing your investment money effectively in different groups. There are 5 main groups of investment in a typical portfolio. They are:

1. **Bonds**. Bonds are sold by the government or by major corporations. Bonds pay a very low fixed interest rate per year, but they are almost completely risk-free. They are often referred to as "T-Bills" or 'T-Bonds", and they usually comprise the conservative portion of a portfolio.

2. **Large Growth Companies**. Stock purchases in large companies/ corporations and banks are good and somewhat safer to invest in because they have a longer track record for performance and they usually pay dividends ($ from profits) to shareholders. Large Growth Companies tend to stay around, earn profits, and grow. They pay a little better than bonds, but they do carry a certain amount of risk. *They are considered the most popular type of investment.*

3. **Value Stocks**. Value stocks are stock purchases in large companies/ corporations who get into financial trouble. Large companies sometimes have bad quarters or bad years. They many actually have a track record of this and it is often due to world economic events and the overall economy. It doesn't necessarily mean they are bad companies. There are many current examples. Just look at the federal bail-outs for most major banks and auto manufacturers. The stock prices for those companies fell up to 90% in 2009-10. People who purchased these Value Stocks when they were low made HUGE profits after the bail-out. Value Stocks are risky, and you have to study each one carefully to manage the risk of investing in them.

4. **Small Business Stock**. Small businesses comprise 90%+ of all businesses in America. Therefore, it's wise to invest part of your savings in them. When their stocks go up for sale it usually means that they are selling those shares to raise money for growth and/or expansion. Growth and expansion usually mean bigger profits, therefore higher stock values. Just the act of selling the stock and people buying it raises the value. These stock purchases have high returns when you invest in the right ones. That's the trick. Buying the right ones. With great potential for profits comes greater risk. Careful choices and LOTS of research are the key.

5. **Small Business Value Stock**. Small Business Value Stocks are stocks that were high at some point and have fallen greatly in value. This is the highest risk investment you can add to a portfolio, but because the cost is relatively low, it is the most potentially profitable stock to purchase. Research, research, and more research is the key. Even then you may buy a fair share of losers in this category. The pay-off is in adding them to your investments despite the risk. The returns on just one winner that recovers its value can offset several others that fail, and they can earn a higher

overall profit than any of your other investments. Investors compare this type of investment to sports betting on a business.

Example Portfolio

This portfolio is based upon an actual $500 investment made in 1924 and managed until 2004 by a very savvy investor who sticks to these 5 basic principles of investing. The point of this is to show just how much a small but smartly diversified portfolio can grow over time.

$500 Invested Into Five Basic Categories with $100 in Each				
1924 $100 Invested	1924 $100 Invested	1924 $100 Invested	1924 $100 Invested	1924 $100 Invested
Government Bonds	Large Growth Company Stocks	Value Stocks	Small Business Stocks	Small Business Value Stocks
2004 $8,000 Return	2004 $194,000 Return	2004 $430,000 Return	2004 $762,000 Return	2004 $3,000,000 Return

The irony in this breakdown of "return on investment", or ROI, for this portfolio is that **Large Growth Company Stocks and Small Business Value Stocks** have approximately the same amount of risk, but have a huge difference in the potential return. Small Business Value Stocks yield over ten times the return of the big stocks, but finding the right ones can be time consuming and difficult for beginners. By using smart diversification you can balance the risks and returns without having to invest time and energy that you may not have.

❖ Principle #3: "Minimize your expenses."

This is as simple as looking at a weight loss plan. You only have two parts to any normal weight loss program, exercise and diet . . . that's it. The crazy part is that the weight loss industry is a multi-billion dollar market yearly. People pay billions to hear simple common sense techniques because they are packaged and marketed to impress and dazzle us. It's the same with investing. Mutual funds and professional money managers like AIG and other Wall Street firms can make big money off of your investments doing things that you can easily do yourself. An S&P 500 Mutual Fund that actually earns 9.1% in a single year may only pay you, the investor, a paltry 3.8% for your money. They keep the balance as their fee. Fees, loads, blah, blah, blah. There are numerous terms to creatively camouflage the ways they find to charge you extra money. It's overhead that you don't need. Minimize your expenses. Go with No-Load Funds and/or Passive Managed Funds.

❖ **Principle #4: "Manage your funds automatically."**

Balance your portfolio automatically, and do it yourself. There are hundreds of online resources, chat rooms, and free help organizations to choose from. Always try to choose INDEX FUNDS. These are funds that have NEVER failed in their history. They are usually low-interest and whole owned investment funds and/or stocks. Dollar Cost Averaging is the next step in managing your funds automatically. You set up your portfolio to buy the same amount of whatever you purchase consistently over time. This means that you also must avoid Financial Paralysis. Financial Paralysis starts when people sell when the markets go down instead of holding on firmly to their investment strategy. Then they start buying again when the markets start to recover. Fear-driven investing like this is a sure way to loser your money. By utilizing Dollar Cost Averaging, you invest daily, monthly, or yearly the same amount of money and in the same way consistently. You also set up this purchasing to buy when the markets go down and sell again when they recover. That's the way to make money from your investments!

❖ **Principle #5: "Choose bonds." When you can. Bonds are *always* the safest investments out there.**

Knowing the risk of loss is the real key to making better choices. Choose government or conservative corporate bonds. Adding bonds to your investment portfolio is a sure way to safeguard your level of risk while investing. Especially when you are starting out. A great way to start is by putting 50% of your money in bonds and the rest into the other 4 types of investments. Bonds limit your potential losses, and proper balance is the key.

Summing it all up

Now you understand the 5 basic principles of investment. The first BIG step is finding money to invest. This can be done as easily as eliminating a few things from your daily spending.

Start saving now!! Quit doing something that costs you money and does nothing for you. Quit smoking, no more Starbucks coffee, no more fast food. Do this, and that $5 per day ($1,850 per year) you were saving turns into $5,000 per year or more. If this money is invested using the 5 principles, it can easily turn into $3,000,000 over 30 years.

Saving and investing money is a habit that will secure financial freedom for anybody who commits to the process.

LESSON 11

FINAL INTERVIEWS

FINAL EXAM

Tips for Lesson:

- ❖ While students are completing their "one-on-one" final interviews, the rest of the students review lessons in a "question and answer" format.

- ❖ After the last student completes their final interview, a test is given. This test covers the Interview process and ends the Employability portion of the course.

Final Interviews

❖ The best way to make this lesson work is to set up as private an area as you can, and conduct an actual interview with each student one at a time.

❖ The rest of the class will be reviewing all previous lessons.

❖ Keep the interviews within a 10-minute each time frame and take notes during the interview to share with the students in front of the entire class.

❖ This allows all of the students to benefit from the interviews and discuss each student's performance while offering praise, helpful hints, or critique.

❖ Twenty students at 10 minutes each will take 200 minutes or 3 hours/20 minutes.

❖ This may cause Lesson 11 to take up two sessions.

❖ Be flexible and fit in elements of other lessons during the interview.

KEEP JOB INTERVIEWS NARROW IN THEIR FOCUS TO AVOID ANY TROUBLE

While most small companies start as one-man shops, a time comes when employees are needed for growth. Asking the right questions during a job interview will help the business owner make the right hire and avoid potential discrimination lawsuits, said Rosa Cantor, president of Creative Human Resources Concepts in Phoenix. She provides a variety of human resource training, from employee handbooks to employee file requirements.

A first step is creating a "pre-application" form, signed by the prospective employee, which gives the employer the authorization to do background checks. Cantor said the form often weeds out applicants who may have something to hide but it can also be good tool. For example, if a job opens up that requires driving; you have permission to check driving records. That's important because of liability issues.

Next is making sure the job interview sticks to questions about the job and skills required for the job, she said.

Avoid questions about age, marital status, children, sexual orientation, health or disabilities. While that may seem obvious, some employers may slip a question about maiden name or family planning, thinking the question is harmless, she said. But they ultimately can be used against the business if a discrimination lawsuit is filed.

If an employee offers personal information about family or health, that should not be viewed as an OK to talk about those issues.

"Say, excuse me. Let's focus on the skills for the job," Cantor says.

"Questions about health are becoming more predominant from both employers and employees," she said. "Employers are concerned about skyrocketing premium costs and employees want to make sure they have good coverage, but those need to be avoided in the interview," she said.

"Also, avoid jotting down personal observations in your interview notes. They can be used against you in a discrimination claim," she said.

Questions that should be asked are:

- ❖ Why are you interested in the job? What to you know about the position?

- ❖ What are your work achievements? Current responsibilities?

- ❖ How do your skills apply to this job?

- ❖ What are your long-term goals if you are selected for the job?

- ❖ What is your definition of a team player? Customer service?

The answers will give the owner an idea of the applicant's commitment and work ethic, Cantor said.

"For small business, every single employee counts. If you don't have the right people, it can be detrimental to your company," she said.

Pre-Release Mail-In Exam and Certificate of Achievement

For inmate students who wish to document their participation in the "From Here to the Streets" Pre-release and Employability Course, the following multiple choice exam is designed to test knowledge regarding pre-release, employability, and the other topics in this course. A score of 85% or better is a passing grade, and will earn the participating student a Certificate of Achievement. Simply record your answers on a separate sheet of paper, enclose a check or money order for the $14.95 processing fee payable to A1info4u Inc., and mail them both to:

Pre-Release Certificate, P.O. Box 24-3664, Boynton Beach, FL 33424

You will receive your certificate in 4 to 6 weeks. Be sure to specify what address you want your certificate issued to. If you do not receive a passing grade, you may re-test one additional time without repaying the processing fee by resubmitting another list of answers. Be sure to record your answers by number; 1-7 multiple choice, 1-30 True or False, and 1-4 Essays. Print clearly and use clean lined paper.

****

Pre-Release and Employability Exam
(Multiple Choice)

1. When should an incarcerated inmate begin to prepare for his or her release?

   a. 12 to 18 months prior to release
   b. 6 months prior to release
   c. Immediately
   d. When a suitable program is available

2. What is the difference between a Transferable Skill and a Personal Skill?

   a. A transferable skill is learned at one job and used at another, and a personal skill is a trait or characteristic that helps in the workplace.
   b. A personal skill is a skill that is learned at one job and used at another, and a transferable skill is a skill that one personally develops at a particular job.
   c. There is no difference; they are both learned skills from previous employment.
   d. Transferable skills are taught and Personal skills you are born with.

3. What is the name of an insurance program for felons that can protect prospective employers from dishonesty or theft in the workplace?

    a. State Farm Ex-offenders Protection Plan
    b. Allstate Felony Coverage
    c. Federal Bonding Program
    d. Ex-offenders Surety Relief Fund

4. What type of mortgage has a payment that can increase after a set period of time?

    a. Flex
    b. Variable
    c. Fixed
    d. Hybrid

5. Which of the following is a question that helps you measure your integrity?

    a. How well do I treat others if I have nothing to gain?
    b. Am I transparent to others?
    c. Am I the same person in the spotlight as when I'm alone?
    d. All of the above

6. Which of these is a way people learn the skills they will need in a trade of their choice while combining both classroom training and job supervision?

    a. On the job training
    b. Apprenticeship
    c. Employment Agency Placement
    d. None of the above

7. Which of the following provide a variety of Small Business Loan opportunities?

    a. FTC
    b. SBA
    c. SEC
    d. One Stop Centers

(True or False)

1. Eye contact is a vital part of the interview process.
2. It is better not to know the history of a company you are applying for.
3. Falsifying information at any stage is grounds for dismissal.
4. Always be prepared for the unexpected during an interview.
5. It is acceptable to criticize your last employer during an interview because they fired you.
6. The purpose of an interview is to allow the employer to get to know you better.
7. Body language is not part of the interview process.
8. During the interview process it is acceptable to smoke if you ask first.
9. A job interview is an opportunity for the applicant to sell himself/herself.
10. You only get one chance to make a first impression.
11. It is permissible to bring a friend to an interview for moral support.
12. Most companies today have background checks before hiring.
13. When discussing your felony conviction don't retry the case or make excuses.
14. It is acceptable to give just give yes or no answers during your interview process.
15. Personal hygiene is not part of the interview process.
16. When the interview is over quickly leave the room.
17. You should send a Thank-You Letter within the first 24 hours after the interview.
18. If you have a dinner interview, it is okay to order alcohol.
19. It is acceptable to interrupt the interview at anytime.
20. You should arrive for your interview no earlier than 15 minutes.
21. Feel free to ask for clarification before answering a question.
22. You do not need to bring anything but yourself to the interview.
23. Crossing your arms in an interview shows that you are interested in the interview.
24. It is okay for you to repeat the question you are asked before answering.
25. Never touch or lean on the interviewer's desk.

26. You should never ask the interviewer questions after the interview is over.

27. Before your interview the most important thing is to practice, practice, and more practice.

28. Know where to go and who to speak to prior to an interview.

29. You do not have to introduce yourself to the interviewer because they already know who you are.

30. You are always in control and have the last word in the interview process.

(Essay)

1. LIST 5 REASONS PEOPLE FAIL TO GET JOBS.

2. LIST 5 REASONS WHY PEOPLE LOSE THEIR JOBS.

3. LIST 5 QUESTIONS YOU COULD BE ASKED DURING AN INTERVIEW.

4. LIST 5 QUESTIONS YOU COULD ASK THE INTERVIEWER.

5. LIST 3 WAYS TO REPAIR YOUR PERSONAL CREDIT.

(Bonus Question)

EXPLAIN IN 250 WORDS OR LESS WHAT THE IMPACT OF THE EXPERIENCES OF ONE'S UPBRINGING HAS UPON ONE'S ABILITY TO MAKE HEALTHY DECISIONS AS AN ADULT (In other words: "If you had observed your parents participating in criminal behavior, what effect might it have on your decision to be involved in similar illegal behavior?)

LESSON 12

REENTRY

Pre-Release / Reentry

This lesson is intended to help you begin the process of re-entering the community. Use your facility's resources and lists of pre-release options, programs, and information for this section. Most agencies have criteria to determine who is eligible for their programs, so you can't just show up on their doorsteps and expect them to have room for you. It's best to write to them before your release to find out their requirements. The agencies will accept ex-offenders, although they may have some restrictions on types of offenses. Find the type of agency that fits your situation and special needs. Don't waste your time writing to a program that can't help you. Agencies are halfway houses and drug/alcohol treatment centers. Information included in this lesson will help you after you are released. Transportation, places for meals, and some special programs are discussed, as well as housing. If you are being paroled, remember to make immediate contact with the parole office and follow all parole conditions completely. They will also give you information about health care and food stamps.

Today a lot of information is available on-line. Contact your local library for information about instructions and free access.

Please note that, some organizations may have moved, changed phone numbers, or may not exist by the time you contact them. Try not to be discouraged. Keep asking until you get the information you need.

Family Issues

The transition back home can be almost as disruptive for the family as when the person first goes to prison. Many adjustments have been made in that person's absence, and families need to learn how to be a family again. Children will have many questions about how things will be different, and it is important for the whole family to discuss what the new rules and routines will be. Each child reacts differently to having a parent return home, and some may still harbor anger or resentment. We strongly recommend family counseling to assist you in this transition. Many formerly incarcerated women have questions about how to regain guardian status. In some cases, the person may have an active file at Child Protective Services (CPS) that they need to clear up. CHILD SUPPORT!!! Many ex-offenders have this issue to deal with, and every situation is unique. Your best strategy is to file for a hearing in front of the judge assigned to your case. They are reasonable and helpful if you show up with a little money in hand, a plan to make continued timely payments, and a willing and humble attitude.

Making a "Personal Game Plan"
For Your Release

Getting out of prison is a stressful experience no matter how prepared you may believe that you are. In effect, you are moving from one type of culture to another. To lessen the shock and increase your odds of success you should draft a personal checklist tailored to your specific needs. Many inmates put this process off or dismiss the notion of writing things down at all. A history professor once said that, "If it's not written down it never happened, and if you don't write things down they never will . . ." This is true in many ways. When a person leaves prison there are hundreds of distractions to derail any well thought out plan. Writing down your plans keeps you focused. It's like making a list to take to the grocery store. You stick to that list; otherwise you end up with a cart full of stuff you really don't need and forget to pick up the things you went for in the first place. "Getting out" is just like that. If you don't create a list, and work through that list, many things simply will not get done.

The Personal Game Plan

Simply put, your game plan is a list of realistic and attainable short term goals. Everybody's long term goals are roughly the same . . . not returning to prison, getting a good job, taking care of or starting a family. It's the specific short term goals we set for ourselves that pave the way to our long term ones. One of the best ways to start is by creating lists that cover each day of your first 2 to 4 weeks after release. Write each list to cover 3 to 4 days at a time.

Remember not to assume you have jobs and other resources waiting for you. Just because somebody promises you something, even if its family, it's not a guarantee. Many ex-inmates re-offend after going home to broken promises. You must make a plan that relies upon you and what you can do. There are many resources available out there. One Stop Career Centers have lists of places to obtain employment, housing, food, clothes, tools, and transportation. Your "Game Plan Checklist" for the first 4 days should look something like this:

Game Plan Checklist

Day 1
- ❖ Call my family
- ❖ Go see my parole officer
- ❖ Check in at my halfway house
- ❖ Set up transportation options (Public, friends, family, etc.)
- ❖ Go and pick up and purchase clothing and hygiene items

Day 2
- ❖ Go to The DMV for my license
- ❖ Go to the Social Security Office for my replacement card
- ❖ Go to the One Stop Center and register for receiving services, set up my Federal Bonding, update my resume, and set up job interviews
- ❖ Set up a free e-mail account

Day 3
- ❖ See my family
- ❖ Set up job interviews
- ❖ Open a checking account
- ❖ Get a copy of my credit report

Day 4

- ❖ Go to job interviews
- ❖ See my children
- ❖ Go to a 12 step or support group meeting
- ❖ Make phone calls and e-mail my networking contacts

Making your plan a Plan for Success

Notice that things like going to the old neighborhood, having a party with old friends, or looking for a date do not make the first list. The hard truth is that if you do not get yourself squared away first before worrying about recreation your odds of violating parole or re-offending go through the roof. This is common sense, and your choice. You may not get everything done on the time table you set, but by crossing things off as you get them done you focus on what's left to do. This process is flexible, too. You can add and delete tasks as you go. The key is writing everything down and gradually and steadily getting things done. Before you know it, you are closer and closer to those long term goals.

A Word about Networking

Networking is developing a pool of people who can help you, provide you with useful information, or even introduce you to others willing to help. Making a list of the names and contact information of everybody who gives you any positive feedback is the beginning of this networking. Your friends, family, clergy, and even prospective employers who liked you during the interview, but couldn't hire you right away are references for you. It's all about who you are now and what you want to do with your future, not just where you've been and how you got there.

Transportation

Owning a vehicle isn't what it used to be. Auto insurance and the rising costs of gas are primary concerns. If you get out of prison and start driving without first having your driver license and car insurance straightened out you will end up back in trouble, and probably lose the vehicle as well. Public transportation . . . the bus, subway, or train is the best way to avoid this. Rates are low and the ride isn't too bad. Choose housing with access to the routes and you will find it easy to get almost anywhere you need to go. Also try to car pool with co-workers or neighbors. Get financially stable before you purchase your own vehicle. Also try bicycling. An adult all-terrain bike is $100.00 assembled and ready to go at any Wal-Mart. Throw on a backpack and water bottle and you're ready to go . . . . It's healthy too!

Identification

- ❖ Birth Certificate
    - ○ Look up the State Bureau of Vital Statistics in the state you were born in. You will be required to pay a fee and provide detailed family information, as well as identification in some cases. All states are different, so do your homework and don't wait until the last minute. Also, don't assume that a copy of your birth certificate is safely tucked away somewhere. If you can't 100% verify its existence and location, apply for a new one.

- ❖ Driver's License
    - ○ Even if you already have had a driver's license, it may be expired or suspended. Contact your local DMV (Division of Motor Vehicles) for times or an appointment to go and get your license checked, re-issued, or reinstated. Be sure to take as many identifying documents as you can just to be safe and prepared. Do not drive until your license is squared away.

Creating Your Personal "Game Plan"

Now that you have seen an example of a personal "game plan", make your own game plan for your first four (4) days after your release from prison. Make sure that you cover all of your bases. You will need to go see your Parole Officer. You will also need all the official documents required to drive and work (Drivers License, Birth Certificate, Social Security Card, etc.) An oversight that many people make is not planning for the time you will need to "decompress" from prison. Make sure that you take some "me time" in all of this. Other short-term goals should include filling out job applications and going to interviews. Whatever your list is, write it down so you can use it as a checklist when you get out.

Day 1

_____
_____
_____
_____
_____

Day 2

_____
_____
_____
_____
_____

Day 3

_____
_____
_____
_____
_____

Day 4

_____
_____
_____
_____
_____

Lists of Acceptable Identifying Documents

LIST A	LIST B	LIST C
Documents That Establish Both Identity And Employment Eligibility	Documents That Establish Identity	Documents That Establish Employment Eligibility
1. U.S. Passport (unexpired or expired)	1. Driver's license or ID card issued by a state or outlying possession of the United States provided it contains a photograph or information such as name, date of birth, sex, height, eye color and address.	1. U.S. Social Security card issued by the Social Security Administration (other than a card stating it is not valid for employment)
2. Certificate of U.S. Citizenship (INS Form N-560 or N-561)	2. ID card issued by federal, state or local government agencies or entities, provided it contains a photograph or information such a name, date of birth, sex, height, eye color and address.	2. Certification of Birth Abroad issued by the Department of State (Form FS-545 or Form DS-1350)
3. Certificate of Naturalization (INS Form N-550 or N-570)	3. School ID card with a photograph	3. Original or certified copy of a birth certificate issued by a state, county, municipal authority or outlying possession of the United States bearing an official seal.
4. Unexpired foreign passport, with 1-551 stamp or attached INS Form 1-94 indicating unexpired employment authorization	4. Voter's registration card	4. Native American tribal document.
5. Alien Registration Receipt Card with photograph (INS Form 1-151 or 1-551)	5. U.S. Military card or draft record	5. U.S. Citizen ID Card (INS Form 1-197)
6. Unexpired Temporary Card (INS Form 1-688)	6. Military dependent's ID card	6. ID Card for use of Resident Citizen in the United States (INS Form 1-179)
7. Unexpired Employment Authorization Card (INS Form 1-688A)	7. U.S. Coast Guard Merchant Mariner Card	7. Unexpired employment authorization document issued by the INS (other than those listed under List A.
8. Unexpired Reentry Permit (INS Form 1-327)	8. Native American tribal document	
9. Unexpired Refugee Travel Document (INS For 1-571)	9. Driver's license issued by a Canadian government authority	
10. Unexpired Employment Authorization Document issued by the INS which contains a photograph (INS Form 1-688B)	10. School record or report card	
	11. Clinic, doctor or hospital record	
	12. Day-care or nursery school record	

Transitional Success Strategies

❖ *Do your homework*: Make as many arrangements for yourself as you can before you get out.

❖ *Give yourself time to adjust*: Don't try to accomplish everything right away. Take time alone or with family and close friends only. Be patient with yourself and know it might take you a while to reach your goals. You may feel depressed or overwhelmed. This is normal—just take some time to heal.

❖ *Ask for help*: There is an answer to every question you have. All you need to do is ask. This does not make you weak . . . it makes you smart. Keep asking until you get the right answer.

❖ *Try to find new playgrounds, playmates, and playthings*: Stay away from the "old neighborhood." Avoid people and places that are associated with your old behaviors. This may even include family members who are still using drugs or are involved in illegal activity. As hard as it may be, you must take care of yourself and surround yourself with people who will affirm your new lifestyle and support you in making positive changes.

❖ *Acquiring clothing*: Many programs will refer their clients to local clothing banks around town. Most of these places will only serve people who are in a program and get a voucher from that program. If you are involved in a housing or counseling program, ask them about a voucher for free clothing. If you are not involved in a program, call Information and Referral and ask for a referral to a clothing bank.

Housing Concerns

Most places will ask you to complete an application and, perhaps, to have an interview. You will probably be asked for certain background information, including a question about felony convictions. You can prepare for the application and interview process by doing the following:

- ❖ Bring along your parole officer's contact information
- ❖ Bring proof of current employment
- ❖ Arrange for 2-3 people to be your personal references. These should be people who know you and who can speak well of you. You may need to provide their contact information to the apartment manager. Speak to these people in advance so that they are prepared to receive a call about you.
- ❖ Make a good impression on the person you speak with by having a presentable appearance—clean clothes and good hygiene are important.
- ❖ Check first to see whether or not you have good credit.

Many property managers like to have tenants who are quiet and respectful of their neighbors, so if this fits your personality and lifestyle it would be an effective point to make during the housing application process. Many apartment managers will claim that they do not house offenders. However, proper attitude and presentation may open the door. Sometimes the nature of the offense makes a difference, for example, they are willing to make an exception if it was a minor, non-violent offense. It is also possible to contact the property owners or management company directly to request an exception be made before you submit the standard application they provide.

Finally . . .

You are not the first to have made a mistake and you won't be the last, but let this be a new chapter in your life. Just remember, the streets still remain the streets and if you seek trouble it will find you. Avoid those old haunts and those old "friends" who are not healthy for you. Break clean with that old environment. This may even include family members who are still using drugs or are involved in illegal activity. As painful as it may be, you must take care of yourself and surround yourself with people who will affirm your new lifestyle and support you in making positive changes. Anticipate problems so they don't overwhelm you. Be patient and take things one step at a time. Prioritize the things that really need to happen (getting a job) and let the rest come when you are ready (finding a new girlfriend or boyfriend). Seek advice and assistance from peers and mentors who seem to be doing it right. Be your own best advocate.

Rights for Convicted Felons

A felony conviction will follow you for as long as you let it. As a convicted felon, you are stripped of some of your Constitutional rights, but you are still a citizen of the United States of America. This means you still are protected by due process clauses contained in the Fifth and Fourteenth Amendments. All convicted felons should be familiar with these articles of the Constitution and your state's laws.

❖ **Right to Vote and Bear Arms**

The moment you are found guilty or plead guilty to a felony, you instantly lose your rights to vote and bear arms (except in Vermont and Maine, where convicted felons and prisoners can still vote). However, in virtually every state, convicted felons may apply for restoration of their rights after completion of their sentence. Most states have simple applications and small filing fees to request the restoration of suffrage and gun rights. Violent convictions, such as assault or rape, will permanently bar your right to bear arms. Visit the website for the court you were convicted in, and the forms will likely be on there for you to print and fill out.

❖ **Right to Own a Passport**

Contrary to popular belief, being a convicted felon does not bar an individual from owning a passport. Granted, if you are still on probation or parole, you will have to get permission from your custodial officer to travel abroad. The primary issues checked by the State Department before issuing passports are citizenship and current state-issued identification.

❖ **Appeals Because of New Evidence**

If you have been sentenced to lifetime probation, and discover new evidence in your case with could exonerate you, a Petition for Federal Writ of Habeas Corpus is how you could potentially clear your name. This option is only available for persons still in custody (including parole or probation) of the agency that convicted them. Federal Habeas Corpus forms are simple to fill out and can be picked up at your nearest U.S. District Court, and there is only a $5 filing fee. You do not need to be a law expert to file one; however, if a federal judge accepts your petition for review, if would be wise to hire counsel.

❖ Fifth and Fourteenth Amendment

The Fifth Amendment guarantees all U.S. citizens (convicted felons or otherwise) the "right to life, liberty, and property" which cannot be deprived without "due process of the law." The Fourteenth Amendment says the same things, but it applies to the states, while the Fifth applies to federal convictions. Nobody can deprive you of your right to appeal any conviction or your right to restore suffrage and gun rights. This would amount to a cause of action for filing a federal lawsuit pursuant to the 1964 Civil Rights Act.

Federal judges "liberally construe" pleadings filed by people representing themselves, so with a little research and dedication, this can be done without a lawyer. There is no need to spend money on things you can easily do yourself. However, for more complex legal issues, retaining a lawyer is a sound practice.

❖ Misconceptions

Everybody makes mistakes and having a felony record does not have to be the end of the world. Many convicted felons go back to school and complete a college degree. Thee only type of conviction that bars individuals from obtaining federal financial aid are drug convictions. Many employers (except for banks) will still hire convicted felons as long as remorse and rehabilitation are shown.

Again, a felony conviction can be the end of your life only if you let it.

References for Keyword Searches

❖ How to apply for a passport
❖ Restoration of Civil Rights Application
❖ States restoring voting rights for ex-convicts

How to Obtain a Passport
For Convicted Felons

The U.S. passport is a document that allows you to travel between countries and identifies you as a U.S. Citizen. Obtaining a passport can be a lengthy process if you're not prepared. A convicted felon applies for a passport in the same way someone without conviction. Being a convicted felon has no bearing on your ability to obtain a passport.

Things you'll need:

- ❖ Passport application form DS-11
- ❖ Proof of citizenship
- ❖ Proof of identity
- ❖ Two passport photos

Obtaining a passport

❖ **Step 1**
Carefully review and fill out a passport application form DS-11. Be sure to read it carefully and ensure all information is correct; will be sworn to it under oath.

❖ **Step 2**
Secure a document proving you are a U.S. citizen. A birth certificate is adequate.

❖ **Step 3**
Proof of personal identity is required to show you are who you say you are and not attempting to commit identity theft. This can be a state issued ID or a driver's license.

❖ **Step 4**
Take two photos for use in your passport. These photos must be two inches by two inches in size and be identical. They must have been taken within the last six months and must have been taken against a white background.

❖ **Step 5**
Locate a U.S. passport processing center and bring all appropriate forms and identifications with you along with the required processing fee.

Tips & Warnings:
- Prepare and apply for your passport early; processing ranges from 4-10 weeks.
- Being a convicted felon does not bar you from obtaining a passport, but someone under probation or parole may not be allowed to leave the country as a condition of parole or probation. Felons are prevented from entering some countries even with a passport. Owing child support arrears of more than $2,500 bars you from obtaining a passport.

Sample Letter:
Halfway House or Program

Your Name
Your Address
City, State, Zip

Today's Date

Agency's Name
Agency's Address
City, State, Zip

Dear Sir or Madam:

My name is _____ and I am currently finishing my
prison sentence at _____. My release date is _____,
and I will have no place to go when I am released.

I am asking that you work with me in advance of my release so that I can have
a place to stay and a program to follow instead of becoming homeless. Please
send me any necessary paperwork and a list of requirements to qualify for your
program so I may collect all that information ahead of time.

I appreciate your assistance, and I eagerly await your reply.

Sincerely,

Your signature

Sample Letter:
Housing Application

Name of Rental Property
Property Manager's Name
Address
City, State, Zip

Today's Date

Your Name
Your Address
City, State, Zip

Dear Property Manager/Landlord:

I am writing this letter to inform you that in _____ (year of conviction) I was convicted of _____, a felony offense. At the time of the crime I was _____ years old, married, and working a full-time job. It was the first and last time I was in trouble with the law.

My decision to _____ (type of crime) was a terrible mistake and it has cost me dearly. Several years of my life have been lost in prison paying for this crime and I am committed to living differently now that I have completed my sentence. I would be happy to answer any questions you have about my conviction during the interview.

I have completed drug rehabilitation, and I am living clean and residing at _____. I hope that you will view me as an individual, and not automatically dismiss this application because of my conviction. My parole officer is _____ and s/he can be reached at _____.

I am a quiet, courteous tenant. I have a full time job and am an active volunteer in the community. If you give me a chance, I know you will find me an excellent tenant. Thank you for your consideration.

Sincerely,

Your signature

Sample Letter
Employment

Dear Prospective Employer:

Please accept this letter of explanation of the lack of information on my employment application about my felony conviction of _____ that occurred on _____.

Because this information is confidential and I am embarrassed over my past mistake, I very much want the opportunity to explain to you in person.

My decision to _____ was a terrible mistake and has cost me dearly. Several years of my life have been lost in prison paying for this crime and I am committed to living differently now that I have completed my sentence. I would like to explain why it will never happen again and why I will be an outstanding employee. To back that up, the U.S. Labor Department is willing, at no cost to you, to post a $5,000 Fidelity Bond with you on my behalf. Additionally, the IRS offers a one-time $2,400 tax credit to employers who hire ex-felons.

I have completed drug treatment/rehabilitation and I am living clean, residing at _____.

I hope you will view me as an individual, and not automatically dismiss this employment application because of my conviction. My parole officer is _____ and can be reached at _____.

Respectfully,

Your signature

What Prisoners Should Know About Social Security

Social Security and Supplemental Security Income (SSI) payments generally are not payable for months that you are confined to a jail, prison or certain other public institutions for commission of a crime. And, you are not eligible for Social Security or SSI payments automatically when you are released.

Who can get Social Security benefits?

Social Security disability benefits can be paid to people who have recently worked and paid Social Security taxes and are unable to work because of a serious medical condition that is expected to last at least a year or result in death. The fact that a person is a recent parolee or is unemployed does not quality as a disability. No benefits are payable for months you are in a jail, prison, or other correctional facility or certain other institutions.

Social security retirement benefits can be paid to people who are 62 or older. Generally, you must have worked and paid Social Security taxes for 10 years to be eligible. Benefits are not paid for the months you have been sentenced to jail, prison, or correctional facility, or confined to certain public institutions for committing a crime. Although you cannot receive monthly Social Security benefit payments while you are confined, your spouse or children can be paid benefits on your record if they are eligible. If you have worked and paid Social Security taxes, survivors benefits also may be paid to certain family members in the event of your death.

Who can get SSI payments?

SSI payments can be paid to people who are 65 or older, or who are blind or disabled and whose income and resources are below certain limits. No benefits are payable for any month throughout which you reside in a jail, prison or certain other public institutions. When you are ready to be released, contact Social Security to apply for SSI so that an SSI payment can be made right after your release if you meet all the requirements.

If you think you qualify for benefits.

In all cases, if you think you may qualify for Social Security or SSI payments, you should contact Social Security to apply for benefits.

Contact them at www.socialsecurity.gov or call toll-free 1-800-772-1213 (for the deaf or hard of hearing, call the TTY number, 1-800-325-0778).

The Ins and Outs of Tapping
Social Security Benefits

Maximize Your Payout

Social Security is under increased scrutiny as the nation's biggest retirement program shows signs it may need an overhaul to extend its life. There are ways to ensure that you're taking every step you can to get the maximum payout. Here are some strategies to put you on the right track.

First, there's What You Pay In

Practically everyone is the U.S. pays 6.2 percent of income, up to $106,800, into the Social Security Trust Fund. Employers match that with another 6.2 percent. In 2011 the employee contribution rate was cut to 4.2 percent, though the employer's share remains at 6.2 percent. For 2012, President Barack Obama has proposed dropping the employee's and employer's contribution to 3.1 percent each. Social Security payments started at 1 percent of income in 1937 and gradually increased until they hit 6.2 percent in 1990. Self-employed workers contribute the full 12.4 percent.

Cost-of-Living Adjustments

When benefits begin, Social Security makes a cost-of-living adjustment based on the percentage increase in the Consumer Price Index. "This is a fairly unique benefit of Social Security", says Merton Bernstein, professor emeritus at Washington University in St. Louis. "There is a tremendous reluctance among other pension funds to offer full cost-of-living adjustments because it is regarded as a burden on the pension." Annual cost-of-living increases have ranged from more than 14 percent in 1908 to 1.3 percent in 1998. Last year marked the first time that there was no adjustment. For 2012, the estimated increase in the Social Security cost-of-living adjustment is 3.5 percent.

Alternative State Plans

When Social Security was enacted in 1935, state and local government employees were excluded from coverage. It was believed that the federal government should not have the authority to tax state and local governments. Today, Social Security is available to state and local government employees but many states, including New York, California and Texas, instead provide alternative plans. Contribution rates and employer matching rates vary. Washington University's Bernstein says that while state plans often provide better returns, public employees who withdraw contributions before retiring forfeit their employers' contribution and greatly reduce their benefit.

Limits on Earnings

If you have reached full retirement age—65 to 67—there is no limit to what you can earn and still keep your Social Security benefits. However, if you get Social Security and are younger than full retirement age you can only earn up to $14,160 a year before you begin to lose benefits. For every $2 you earn above that amount, Social Security will deduct $1 in benefits.

Waiting's Big Benefits

The Social Security benefits you receive can differ greatly depending on the age at which you start taking them. Say you were due to receive $1,000 a month at age 66. If you claim at age 62, your first opportunity to start claiming benefits, your monthly payment will be $750. If you wait until you're 70, the monthly benefit rises to $1,320—an increase of 76 percent. Keep in mind that after you reach full retirement age, which is 65 to 67, you get an increase of 8% for every additional year you wait to claim, until age 70.

The Marriage Benefit

If your spouse had earned a bigger Social Security benefit than you, you can claim 50 percent Social Security benefits on your spouse's income—as long as that amount would be more than your own Social Security payments would be if you were to claim. You can then wait until after you reach full retirement age to switch to your own Social Security claim, thereby receiving the maximum payout.

The Twice-Divorced Benefit

You can collect on your former spouse's Social Security benefits as long as you were married for at least 10 years, are 62 or older and the benefit you'd receive from your ex-spouse is greater than the benefit you'd receive from your own work. If you remarry, you lose that benefit unless your second spouse dies or the marriage ends in divorce. In that case, you can claim benefits from the ex-spouse who would generate the greatest payment.

Double Dipping

If you recently started collecting Social Security but now wish you'd waited so you would receive a higher monthly benefit, you can turn back time. As long as it has been under 12 months since you claimed, you can pay back the benefits your received and the government won't charge you taxes. If you have already paid taxes, you can request a refund. Then you can do it all again later, when your payout will be higher.

From the Department of Veterans Affairs Compensation & Pension Service

Can a Veteran Receive VA Benefits while in Prison?
VA can pay certain benefits to veterans who are incarcerated in a Federal, state, or local penal institution. The amount depends on the type of benefit and reason for incarceration.

How Will Your Imprisonment Effect the Payment of:
VA Disability Compensation?
Your monthly payment will be reduced beginning the 61st day of your imprisonment for a felony. If your payment before incarceration was greater than the 10% rate, your new payment will be at the 10% rate. If you were getting the 10% rate before, your new payment will be half the 10% rate.

VA Disability Pension?
If you are imprisoned in a Federal, state, or local penal institution as the result of conviction of a felony or misdemeanor, such pension payment will be discontinued effective on the 61st day of imprisonment following conviction.

Are You Eligible for VA Medical Care while Imprisoned?
Incarcerated veterans do not forfeit their eligibility for medical care; however, current regulations restrict VA from providing hospital and outpatient care to a veteran who is an inmate in an institution when that agency has a duty to give the care or services. VA may provide care once the veteran has been unconditionally released. Veterans interested in applying for enrollment should contact the nearest VA facility upon their release.

Can Your Dependent(s) Receive Any Money Not Paid While You Are Imprisoned?
VA can take all or part of benefits you are not receiving and apportion it to your spouse, child, and dependent parents based on need. Contact a VA regional office to apply. They will be asked to provide income information as part of the application process.

When Will Benefits Be Resumed?
Your compensation or pension benefits shall be resumed the date of release from incarceration if the Department of Veterans Affairs receives notice of release within 1 year following release. VA may schedule you for a medical examination to see if your disability has improved. Visit or call your local VA regional office for assistance.

Note: You are considered released from incarceration if you are paroled or participating a work release or halfway house program. For more information, call 1-800-827-1000 or visit www.va.gov.

LESSON 13

SMALL BUSINESS BASICS AND ENTREPRENEURSHIP

Introduction to Entrepreneurship

Everybody reading this has probably thought of being their own boss at least once. Many of you have attempted this. Some of your may have even been successful once or twice. Entrepreneurship isn't for everybody, though. It takes more work and discipline than the best hard working productive employee could ever bring to their job.

Entrepreneurship by definition is the sum of several very specific traits and abilities. Terms like self-starter, highly motivated, creative thinker and problem solver are only a few of them. The worst aspect of this dynamic is just how many people truly believe they have what it takes to be an entrepreneur, but are woefully misinformed or ignorant to the most relevant requirements. Topping the long list of abilities and traits necessary is **Personal Integrity.** The rest of the list is more technical and systemic rather than philosophical. Simply stated, entrepreneurship is a lifestyle, not a job. In this section you will learn most of the basics and many will (hopefully) realize whether or not they have what it takes, or if they need to reassess their goals. It's not black and white, though. You may realize you're coming up short, but also learn what you need to do about it. It's as personal a decision as marriage or raising children. Truth be told, many entrepreneurs spend far more time with their ventures than they do with their families. This kind of sacrifice and many others are just part of the discipline of entrepreneurship.

A final word on this introduction to entrepreneurship, small businesses, startups, etc. No matter what type business ventures you are interested in, there is one basic, yet critical, skill you have to develop, hone, and utilize. This skill is **Networking**. Networking is the way we reach out to the world around us and find potential partnerships, resources, and mutually beneficial relationships. Networking is not looking for handouts or freebies. In order to be effective in your networking you will have to approach potential partners or resources with something of value. This could be as simple as offering your own time, physical labor, or material resources (tools, vehicles, etc) to your potential partners for their use. Even if you believe the offer is unnecessary, it still establishes who you are and what your own level of personal integrity is.

For those of you who will seek venture capital (money) from investors, you always offer a percentage of ownership and/or royalty incentives. By coming empty handed you discredit your true motivations and equate them to greed, manipulation, or usurious behavior.

Small Business/Entrepreneurial Lesson

The key to success in any business or financial venture starts with INTEGRITY. The simple truth is that integrity must be present in all aspects of your life or life itself fails before it can ever truly begin. As one man said . . .

"Healthy adulthood is reached when you choose to quit believing your own lies and live in integrity. It is the only way we can be if we want to have truly successful and fulfilling life."

—John Crosby, 2007

****

QUESTIONS TO HELP YOU MEASURE YOUR INTEGRITY

❖ How well do I treat people if I gain nothing?

❖ Am I transparent with others?

❖ Do I role-play based on the person(s) I'm with?

❖ Am I the same person in the spotlight as I am when I'm alone?

❖ Do I quickly admit wrongdoing without being pressed to do so?

❖ Do I put people ahead of my personal agenda?

❖ Do I have an unchanging standard for moral decisions, or do circumstances determine my choices?

❖ Do I make difficult decisions, even when they have a personal cost attached to them?

❖ When I have something to say about people, do I talk to them or about them?

❖ Am I accountable to at least one other person for what I think, say, and do?

Business Ownership

> **Do you want to be your own boss?**
> **Do you want financial independence?**
> **Do you want to fully use your skills and knowledge?**

- ❖ First you need to determine what business is right for you.
- ❖ Identify the niche your business will fill.
- ❖ Is my idea practical and will it fill a need?
- ❖ What is my competition?
- ❖ What is my business advantage over existing firm?
- ❖ Can I deliver a better quality service?
- ❖ Can I create a demand for my business?

Choosing your business structure

- ❖ Sole Proprietorship—most common
- ❖ General Partnership
- ❖ Limited Partnership
- ❖ "C" Corporation—A legal entity, shareholders, directors and officers. The most complex!
- ❖ Subchapter "S" Corporation—taxed as a partnership
- ❖ "LLC" Limited Liability Company—LLC owners risk only their investment, personal assets are not at risk.

Writing a Business Plan

Preparing a business plan forces you to think through every aspect of your business. As you grow your business plan will help you keep track of the details and make sure the business is progressing as you intended.

Marketing

- ❖ Products and services offered
- ❖ Identify your market, its size and location.
- ❖ Explain how your product or service will be advertised and marketed
- ❖ Explain the pricing strategy.
- ❖ Financial
- ❖ Explain your source and the amount of initial capital.
- ❖ Develop a monthly operating budget for the first year.
- ❖ Develop a monthly-expected return on investment and cash flow.
- ❖ Income and balance sheets for 2 years.
- ❖ Discuss who will maintain accounting records.
- ❖ Discuss "what if" statements.

Operations

- ❖ Explain how the business will operate on a day-to-day basis.
- ❖ Discuss hiring, personnel procedures
- ❖ Cover insurance, lease or rental agreements etc.
- ❖ Discuss equipment necessary for the business, and how to acquire it.

****

Do You Have What It Takes To Own Your Own Business?

Before we go on let me throw in a proverb: *"Laziness leads to poverty, hard work makes you rich."*

- ❖ Who plans to work for someone else and get that steady paycheck every Friday?
- ❖ Who wants to be his/her own boss?
- ❖ Do you want financial independence?
- ❖ Do you want to fully use your skills and knowledge?

I'll tell you right now, I have a bias in favor of being self-employed.

Why?

❖ I want the power to decide my future.

❖ I want the power to create.

❖ I have the belief that if I am committed, if I am passionate, honest, sincere, and have an absolute, never ending persistence, I will succeed. I'll have the opportunity to help people and provide jobs.

❖ Through honesty and integrity I will earn a good reputation and respect.

❖ I want to learn the power of decisions. I believe it's our decisions, not the conditions or our lives, that determine our destiny.

❖ I want to have more control over my income.

Step #1—Start assessing your gifts and abilities

Take a long, honest look at what you are good at, and what you're not good at. Every one of you has dozens of hidden abilities and gifts that you don't know you've got.

Also recognize your limitations. Nobody is good at everything. Right now start to utilize the abilities and gifts God has given you.

Running your own business is not for everyone. Many people are better suited as an employee rather than an employer . . . For me it's being an entrepreneur.

Step #2—Setting Goals

Goals take you beyond your limits to a world of unlimited potential. The most important key to goal setting is to find a goal big enough to inspire you, something that will cause you to unleash your potential. In order to truly find inspiration and achieve those impossible goals, we must change our belief systems about what we're capable of achieving. You should make a list of clearly defined goals for the results you will produce in your life emotionally, physically, spiritually, and financially.

Step #3—Live the Dream

Don't go through life putting off your joy and happiness. If we decide to be happy now, we'll automatically achieve more. How much would you like to earn?

$23,000 a/year	$12.00 a/hr.
$38,000 a/year	$20.00 a/hr.
$58,000 a/year	$30.00 a/hr.
$100,000 a/year	$50.00 a/hr.
$200,000 a/year	$100.00 a/hr.

The key to achieving goals:

Motivation

Change your limiting beliefs

Emotional mastery

Physical mastery

Financial mastery

Time management mastery

Step #4—Making the Decision

I'm not sharing these lessons with you to say that I have all the answers or that my life has been perfect or smooth. I've certainly had my share of challenging times. But through it all, I've managed to learn, persist, and continually succeed throughout the years.

Also, living my lifestyle may not be the answer for you. My dreams and goals may not be yours.

Together we will begin a journey of discovery and the actualization of our deepest and truest potentials. Life is a gift, and it offers us the privilege, opportunity, and responsibility to give something back by becoming more.

It's Time to Identify Your Passions
What Motivates You?
What Interests You?

Is it the latest video game? Is it the new style of clothing to hit the streets? Think about the things that catch your eye and grab your attention. If you love what you are doing, it's not really "working". Not in the conventional way we normally think of a job. As you read this book and decide what you want to try, be sure to choose things that you are going to want to do.

One of the best ways to figure out how a hobby or an interest can create a job or a business is to go visit the office or location this activity takes place. This may sound crazy, but it really works. Everything you enjoy doing has a business aspect attached to it. You may have to purchase memberships, pay fees, buy equipment, and pay for related expenses like transportation, food, or lodging. It doesn't matter what you do. Skating, texting, sports, reading—everything costs money and somebody profits from it. The good news is that you can learn to profit from your interests. This concept is at the heart of what we want you to learn. The rest is teaching you how to act on this information and make it work for you. In the pages that follow, you will learn how to do just that. The primary technique used is networking. Networking is covered in great detail later, but getting out and meeting people is the key.

Plan out every hour of your life . . .

Write a schedule for your entire week that covers all of your time. Be sure to include at least eight hours of sleep, time for exercise, study time, and travel time that covers to and from wherever you go. This is how good "Time Management" starts in your life. You start good habits now and they become your foundation for every part of your future.

Writing down your plans keeps you focused. It's like making a list to take to the grocery store. You stick to that list; otherwise you end up with a cart full of stuff you really don't need and forget to pick up the things you went for in the first place. "Planning out your life" is just like that. If you don't create a list, and work through that list, many things simply will not get done. One of the best ways to start is by creating lists that cover each day of your life right down to hours spent on whatever. You may not get everything done on the time table you set, but by crossing things off as you get them done you focus on what's left to do. This process is flexible, too. You can add and delete tasks as you go. The key is writing everything down and gradually and steadily getting things done.

Small Business Ownership Questionnaire

Before you decide to open a business, there are seven (7) questions you need to be able to answer:

1. Why do you want to start a business?

2. What is the industry like?

3. What is your Business Plan?

4. How will you fund your Business Plan?

5. How will you market your business?

6. How many people will you need to operate your business?

7. What are the legal and tax implications of your business?

If you cannot answer these questions, then opening your business may prove to be difficult. You can find all of these through the Small Business Association (SBA).

T.N.V.

By Joseph L. Chiappetta Jr.

Business theories and principles are plentiful and sometimes redundant. You can find hundreds of books that claim to have the essential information and models for your success. They offer a wide variety of commentary saying roughly the same things about a specific area of interest while customizing the lessons with their own step-by-step procedures and advice. The following theory is a formula that has been crafted from 25 years of experience and research.

For many years I've looked around for "Big Ideas" and "Big Wins". Many times I have thought of something unique or promising, but couldn't put it together for one reason or another. Then years or months later I have seen my idea on the cover of one magazine or another being hailed as a multi-million dollar winner! I believe that most of us have had similar experiences once or twice during our lives. One day I was grieving over one of these "almost could've been mine" ideas when I decided to examine this phenomena more closely. What I came up with was a simple explanation in the form of three words . . . Timing, Niche, and Venue . . . TNV for short.

Timing

It's almost a cliché these days . . . "Everything in life is about timing." You meet that perfect someone only when one of you is seeing somebody else or already married . . . You see the perfect deal come along only when you can't afford it . . . Timing. Timing in business ventures or new ideas can be a bit confusing, though. Sometimes you have to wait and other times you must defy the odds and push forward.

Niche

Niche is another word for specialty or forte. Even if your dream is a hot dog cart, you had better make it stand out among the hundreds of others you're competing with. During the early 1990's in Florida, some girls wearing thongs sold 10 dollar hot dogs on street corners and well traveled roadsides. These events hit the national news, and though short-lived, these ventures put many young women through college or helped them purchase new homes. In the 1980's the classic "Members Only" jackets sold for $100 or more in the best stores . . . Only a few years later they sold for $9.99 at flea markets. Starbucks, Google, and Microsoft are three giants who are constantly setting trends and creating new products. Still, no matter how unique or special something is, you have got to find the best way and most effective place to market and sell it.

Venue

This is where you go to see it, do it, or buy it. Typically this term is used when discussing entertainment, but it also works for your new idea. You have your idea at the perfect time; you have improved upon it to make it special, now you have to "put the rubber on the road". Venue is where you make that happen. For most businesses venue comes down to "brick and mortar" or "website". There are dozens of ways to set up hundreds of different storefronts. There are hundreds of different website layouts and an infinite number of ways to further customize those. With the task of choosing from so many options, finding an effective venue can be like searching for a needle in a haystack.

The Bottom Line

The only stupid questions are the ones left unasked. Asking questions will reinforce your confidence and fix potential problems before they occur. Many entrepreneurs are unsure who or where to ask. One excellent resource is your local Chamber of Commerce. This is a club that allows you to network with hundreds of other business owners. Another great place to go is the Small Business Association and their many free workshops. The byproduct of this networking is help in formulating and asking relevant questions that will ultimately help you analyze your own unique Timing, Niche, and Venue. Recently reviewed several companies and applied my formula of Timing, Niche, and Venue to their successes or failures. In every business, product, or service I found the combination of these three factors played the most important role in their performances. Like tumblers falling into place in a lock, each of the TNV factors had been utilized to their greatest benefit. Bear in mind that there are no guarantees in business and that risks are always present. All you can do is manage those risks to the best of your ability. Below are a series of questions drafted to help you apply TNV to your own venture:

- ❖ Why is the timing right for you to try this?
- ❖ Why is the timing right for the venture itself to work?
- ❖ What is so special or unique about what you want to accomplish?
- ❖ How does what you plan to do stand out among other similar products, services, or ideas?
- ❖ Why have you chosen the specific venue(s) in your plan?
- ❖ What kind of facility(s) or market(s) do you plan to utilize, and why?
- ❖ After answering these questions are you still confident in your plans?
- ❖ How does the sum of the answers to the preceding questions tie together with regards to your original vision of your plans?
- ❖ Do your own TNV components support your confidence?

Entrepreneurial Exercise
Using Your Skills to Open and Operate Your Own Business

Opening a Small Business

When people want to start a Small Business: they have to spend several days doing the basic requirements with regard to licensing, banking, and documenting their business to make it "real" and viable. This finished business entity will consist of at least the following elements:

- ❖ Business Plan
- ❖ Business Name Registration
- ❖ EIN (Employer Identification Number)
- ❖ State and/or County License
- ❖ Physical Business Address
- ❖ Website / E-mail
- ❖ Minimal Operating Expenses
- ❖ Articles of Incorporation (if you are filing)
- ❖ Bank Account(s)
- ❖ Tax Collection Permit
- ❖ Business Phone Service
- ❖ Basic Business Stationery

There are also the installation waiting periods, new account restrictions, and other assorted delays that can make the above elements take several weeks to accomplish. Once these various tasks are completed, the company will be "new" and by that standing, not be eligible for Net 30 Business Credit, Revolving Credit Lines, and Preferred Customer Status at the Bank. Once this "new" company is 1-2 years old, it will be listed in trade publications, Nationwide Directories, and also be listed with Dun and Bradstreet. Then, and only then, will this business be able to stand on its own and be recognized in the business community at large. For individuals, corporations, or partnerships that plan to do retail sales and services, this 1-2 years can be full of obstacles and restrictions that not only force them to rely on their own personal credit, but also deny them access to programs and benefits that other "established" companies are using on a regular basis. Many people purchase an existing business to avoid these various restrictions and waiting periods. Choose your business and make a list of what you will need to do to get things started. Use the above information as a starting point.

*Note to Teachers / Facilitators: Use your own experiences to explain the many details involved in opening and running a business.

Your Business Structuring Choices

Entity	Control	Liability	Tax	Year-End	Continuity
Sole Proprietorship	You have complete control	You are completely liable	You report all income and expense on your personal tax return	Calendar year end	Business terminates with your death
General Partnership	Each partner, including you, can enter into contracts and other business agreements	You are totally liable for all business debts including your partners' share	You report your share of partnership income on your personal tax return	Must be the same as the majority interest tax year, or principle partners'. If neither, must be calendar	Partnership terminates on death or withdrawal of any partner
Limited Partnership	General partners control the business	General partners are totally liable—limited partners are liable for only the amount of their investment	Partnership files annual tax returns—General and Limited partners report their income or loss on their personal tax returns. Losses may be subject to limitations.	Must be same as the majority interest tax year, or principal partners'. If neither, must be calendar	Partnership does not dissolve with death of a limited partner buy may dissolve with death of a general partner unless the partnership agreement states otherwise
Limited Liability Company	Owners or members have the authority	Owners or members are not liable for business debts	Rules vary dependent on the state—"Check the Box" allows election of treatment	Rules vary dependent on the state—"Check the Box" allows election of treatment	Rules vary depending on the state—In some states the company will dissolve upon the death of an owner or member
Corporation C Corp	Shareholders appoint Board of Directors which appoints officers who have the most authority	Shareholders risk only the amount of their investment in the corporation's stock	Corporation pays its own taxes—Shareholders' pay taxes on dividends received	Any month end. Personal service Corp must use calendar	The corporation stands alone as a legal entity—It can survive the death of owner, officer, or shareholder
Subchapter S	Shareholders appoint Board of Directors which appoints officers who have the most authority	Shareholders risk only the amount of their investment in the corporation's stock	Shareholders report their share of the corporate profit or loss on their personal tax return	Calendar year	The corporation stands alone as a legal entity—It can survive the death of owner, officer, or shareholder

Licensing Questions to Consider

Do You Have A Home-Based Business?

A home-based business must comply with the same license and permit requirements as a business located at a commercial site. This includes applicable sales tax licenses, business or occupational licenses, trade or professional certifications or licenses. In addition, home-based businesses must comply with residential zoning and homeowners association rules. One of the first steps you should take to plan a home-based business is to contact the planning and zoning office of your city (or county, if you are outside the city limits). Next, check the rules for your homeowners association or the deed restrictions on your property to be sure your business activities will be in compliance. Some of the more acceptable businesses for home-based operations involve functions such as personal computer services and other clean, quiet enterprises that are more or less "invisible" to neighbors. Other usually acceptable home-based businesses include those in which the entrepreneur's office is located in the home, but all the contacts are made at other locations.

Other considerations:
- Check with city/county zoning regarding rules prohibiting a business with employees or street traffic.
- Check with your accountant regarding state and federal income tax deductions for home office space.
- Check with your insurance agent about additional insurance needs.

Do You Need To Contact Planning And Zoning?

The Planning, Zoning, and/or Development Services Departments of the city and county in which your business is (or will be) located may have restrictions and/or requirements that affect your business. Please contact these offices for specific information. The telephone numbers can be found in the Blue Pages of your local telephone book or by using http://www.dexon-line.com/.

Are You Doing Business In More Than One City?

If your business is located in one city and does business in another city, you may need a license (business, occupational, sales tax) for the additional city. In addition, if your business activity is sales taxable, taxation collections may need to be paid directly to the city in which you are doing business. Please contact each city/town in which you are conducting business.

Caution: 5 Things to Avoid
With a Small Business

Franchise Caution
There are things you should be doing to get your business up and running like a pro; get active on Twitter, Facebook, and Crowd Funding, connect with people in your field, network, etc. It seems that if you're working hard and doing everything possible, you'll gain success. But, there are things that any entrepreneur should avoid doing, things that will actually hurt your company.

Share the Wealth!
Idea wealth, that is. Many entrepreneurs are too scared to talk about an idea for fear somebody will steal it! In more cases than not, nobody has the time, energy, resources or PASSION to turn that idea into a reality. Got an idea? Tell people about it! You'll be shocked at some of the great feedback you get.

Not Having a Business Plan
Having a business plan is like having a road map. Many people do not have one, and seem to be going nowhere. Create and implement one, and the road to success becomes clearer, and more and more opportunities for my business will come your way.

Family "Help"
An entrepreneur's biggest mistake is accepting help from family, particularly in the form of lawyer, accountant or partner. Entrepreneurs must separate themselves from the business. You need experts that will focus on the success of the business instead of taking care of you. Enjoy family dinners and events without your business team in tow.

Avoiding a Closed Mindset
The entrepreneur needs to have an open mindset—be willing to fail—in order to be able to move forward. If something is difficult, don't give up. Push through until you overcome it. Having an open mindset can make a huge difference for any entrepreneur.

Making Exceptions to the Rules
We strive to treat everyone fairly and the same. But there are times you'll be tempted to let someone talk you into doing things you can't do for everyone. Before you know it, small chores multiply, and others want special favors; on it goes. Set boundaries.

Actions Before You Quit Your Day Job

Too many eager entrepreneurs leave their salaried jobs too soon. They abandon their day jobs with only a vague notion of what they want as new business owners. They know the lifestyle advantages of why they want to startup, but not what they want to startup. When business owners start companies without a clear path to revenue generation, they are at high risk for failure. By the time they figure out their business plan and do all the administrative duties associated with business set up, they run out of personal savings. This beat-the-clock cash management challenge can overwhelm just about anyone.

One way to minimize startup risks is to do as many time-consuming administrative duties and research projects a possible before cutting off the salaried paycheck. Here are five pre-startup action steps:

❖ Select business names that don't violate existing trademarks. Good business and product name selections should involve a search for trademark conflicts. Entrepreneurs can limit their exposure by visiting the U.S. Trademark Electronic Search System (TESS). All searches are free. (www.uspto.gov)

❖ Get your financial house in order. Before leaving your day job, set aside extra savings. Correct errors on credit reports and improve credit scores. Business owners with good personal credit get better deals on small business loans, equipment leases, credit card services for e-commerce operations, etc.

❖ Organize your company structure. Will you startup be a sole proprietorship, a limited liability company, a partnership, S-corporation, C-corporation? This is a fundamental question that will determine taxes you will pay on business profits and personal income. It takes time to understand your options plus put in place board members and advisers who can help advance your business interests.

❖ Research health insurance. Before you quit your job, revisit your employer's benefits literature. Under federal COBRA regulations, if you work for a company with more than 20 employees you may be able to continue coverage for 18 months provided you pay the entire cost of coverage.

❖ Consider tactical employment. Would you rather learn about costly business problems on someone else's dime, or experience the pain all by yourself? One way to avoid startup mistakes is to find "tactical employment". These are temporary, part- or full-time jobs to improve expertise and generate extra income. If, for example, your dream is to one day start a craft brewery, work in a beer house first to learn the fine points of manufacturing, pricing, inventory management and distribution. There are risks to moonlighting; entrepreneurs who intend to compete with current employers or develop patentable technologies should understand their legal risks and obligations. Moonlighting entrepreneurs should always work at their business completely off premises to avoid legal conflicts.

One Page Business Plan for:
"Innovative Development Solutions"

Vision

Within the next two years, Innovative Development Solutions will become an effective and profitable Business Incubation and Start-Up Business Consultation Service.

Mission

We will implement a small business incubation program that dovetails perfectly into today's economic crisis. Our services will stimulate economic growth and consumer confidence through the development of ore new businesses. Every new business upon its opening will create new jobs, the use of existing business services, and a measurable bolstering of consumer confidence.

Objectives

- Launch our Start-Up by May 2009
- Generate gross income of $240,000 by the end of our first year.
- Increase revenues to $400,000 by the end of year two.
- Develop our concept into a Franchise Opportunity by the end of year three

Strategies

- Share our success stories with the media to educate, recruit, and further develop our client base.
- Enlist key community leaders and business owners to develop new and productive networking opportunities.
- Cultivate relationships with other organizations and franchisors that have common goals and resources to offer our current and future clients.

Plans

- Complete our 2 Year Plan by May 2011.
- Launch Start-Up and Implementation of our Marketing Plan by May 2009.
- Meet our financial obligations by May 2010.
- Facilitate the opening of 100 new businesses by May 2011.

Innovative Development Solutions
2009 Start Up

The IDS Start Up is a small business incubation program that dovetails into today's economic crisis. In a failing economy or recession what truly stimulates economic growth is consumer confidence and spending. The key to creating confidence is through the development of new businesses. Every new business upon its opening creates new jobs, use of existing business services, and a bolster of consumer confidence.

Our plan creates the above-mentioned dynamic and targets large groups of high value skilled workers. Thousands of such employees have been laid off in the current phase of downsizing and reorganization this year. We will create new jobs for this workforce by launching new business ventures for them. Our clients will be employed by corporations they own. The start-up funding we will arrange for them will provide stable income, health insurance, and the potential to profit directly from their own work product.

The failure rates for new businesses are high. Our clients will have a greater success rate through our unique system of using proven franchise opportunities, those highly rated by business profiling services such as *Entrepreneur Magazine.* Every franchisor has a vested interest in the success of its franchisees, provides training and support, and has a proven system for success. By matching a preferred start-up opportunity with a franchise for our clients we create the proverbial "Best Case Scenario" in launching a new business. IDS will have 10-15 carefully selected franchise opportunities for our clients to choose from, and we will have a close working relationship with each of these franchisors.

The actual services IDS provides to its clients include:

- ❖ Business Selection Counseling
- ❖ Business Start-Up Management
- ❖ Multiple Income Stream Development
- ❖ One Full Year of Onsite Support

The fee for our services is factored into the Start-Up Funding (a loan or venture capital investment). This concept is unique and separates us from many other so-called small business consultants. We only receive payment as part of the start-up funding itself. We have a vested interest in our client's success. A fee of $10,000 is charged for our services to each new business we help create.

A qualified client can walk into our office and be earning a paycheck working for a business he or she actually owns in as little as 4 weeks.

Because of our program's massive income potential we will meet our financial obligations within the first 18 months. Our projected number of new clients in our first year of operation is 2 per month. This will be a total of 24 completed transactions, which amounts to $240,000 gross income. It only takes 3 to 5 working days to draft a business plan, open a corporation, and activate one of our Start-Up Ventures. The funding for each business will take approximately 3 to 8 weeks. Once our offices are fully operational and our management team has a chance to maximize our efforts, we will be able to nearly double these projections for year two.

IDS Financial Requirements

Innovative Development Solutions will require $352,500 in start-up capital. Owners' contribution will include $122,500 in the form of equipment, software, and labor. The balance of $230,000 will be acquired through either a loan or venture capital investment. This money will be used for operating expenses/ overhead to carry the company through its first year of operation.

The break-down of how the $230,000 loan will be spent over the first year is as follows:

- 4 Employee Positions @ $35,000 ($140,000)
- 12 Month Office Lease ($6,000)
- Furniture ($2,000)
- Legal Expenses ($2,500)
- Equipment ($3,500)
- Marketing Expenses ($15,500)
- Utilities (Internet, Phone, Etc.) ($12,000)
- Office Supplies ($6,000)
- Insurance (Health Plan Co-pay, Business, Etc.) ($15,000)
- Vehicle Expenses ($12,000)
- Consultants ($4,500)
- Memberships ($1,200)
- Miscellaneous Expenses ($9,800)

The IDS $122,500 contribution for the first year is as follows:

- 2 Management Positions @$45,000 ($90,000)
- Equipment and Software already purchased ($15,000)
- R&D Expenses already paid ($10,000)
- Miscellaneous Start-Up Expenses already paid ($7,500)

Sample One Page Business Plan
Not-for-Profit Organization
From The One Page Business Plan Company

Vision	Build BAEA into a nationally recognized micro-enterprise organization with an extensive greater San Francisco Bay Area network of entrepreneurial support groups providing nationally recognized products, programs and services to entrepreneurs, small business owners, and partner organizations.

Mission	Create viable businesses and successful entrepreneurial leaders through networking, support and connection to resources.

Objectives	• Increase membership from 150 to 300 by 12/31. • Launch 2 networks by 6/30 and add 3 more networks by 12/31. • Generate $8,0000 from entrepreneurial programs, events and products in this FY • Host 3 regional network events with at least 50 attendees each and generate $4,000. • Increase low-income members to 25 and minority members 25% by 3/20. • Award 5 scholarships totaling $1,300 in current FY. • Recognize 10 entrepreneurs for outstanding business growth & community service.

Strategies	• Use public relations and media to share successes, educate, recruit and fund. • Market and sell BAEA endorsed products and services nationally. • Collaborate with nation micro-enterprise organizations in nation awareness programs and funding. • Establish BAEA center to create long-term community presence and financial asset base. • Enlist key community leaders and businesses to launch and develop new networks. • Attract/retain low-income entrepreneurs by offering scholarships funded by corporate sponsors. • Utilize multi-lingual/cultural programs to attract minority entrepreneurs. • Package successful BAEA programs and products to sell to other micro-enterprise organizations. • Use technology to manage growth, streamline operations, delivers programs, and sell products.

Plans	• Complete 5-years Strategic Pan by 4/30. • Complete funding plan by 6/30. • Hire executive director by 12/31. • Expand board of directors from 4 to 7 by 11/15. • Develop BAEA product and service marketing plan by 3/31. • Develop 2-year network expansion plan by 6/30. • Launch sales/marketing plan of One Page Business Plan by 7/10. • Implement PR Plan by 8/20.

(Sample Non-Profit Executive Summary)

✶✶✶✶✶✶✶✶✶✶✶✶✶✶✶✶✶✶✶✶✶✶✶✶✶✶✶✶✶✶✶✶✶✶✶

Transitional Reentry Solutions
TRS Reentry Initiative—2 Year Intensive Release Program

Executive Summary

❖ *Project Title:*
TRS Reentry Initiative

❖ *Contact Person:*
Jeanne C. Reynolds, Founding Director, Gold Canyon Heart & Home

❖ *Applicant Information:*
Gold Canyon Heart & Home, an Arizona 501c3 Non-Profit Organization

❖ *Mission Statement:*
The TRS Reentry Initiative will provide intensive full-service transitional support for 100 soon-to-be-released offenders in Arizona which will result in a 90%+ success rate among the selected participants.

❖ *Problem Statement:*
Recidivism among prison inmates releasing back into our communities is approximately 65-85% nationally each year. Over 90% of those re-offenders do so within their first year after release. For inmates under 25 years of age the percentage of recidivism is over 95%. Simply offering incarcerated offenders programming, education, and treatment is not enough to impact this problem.

❖ *Project Summary:*
The TRS Reentry Initiative will select 1000 qualified participants to receive 2 years of full-service transitional support. This support is broken down into one year prior to release and one year after release. The first year includes one-on-one mentorship from certified peer mentors who guide the participants through carefully chosen evidence-based classes and programs. Participants will also receive financial education which includes: bank accounts through Prisoner Assistant, Inc., active credit repair and restoration/creation, and employability support which includes resume building and pre-release job interviews and placement.

Upon release the second year of support begins with housing in a 2-3 bedroom home with utilities and rent paid for 90 days. Employment, health insurance, transportation, educational opportunities, pre-paid legal services, and continued mentoring will take place throughout year two. The key to our success is the constant one-on-one support from peer mentors and the complete financial and employment support upon release. Instead of only substance abuse programming or religion as the main focus, the TRS Reentry Initiative targets the main causes of recidivism. These are desperation and fear due to the lack of food, housing, and employment.

❖ *Expected Results:*
The Arizona Department of Corrections spends approximately $35,000 per year to keep an offender in custody with a 65-85% recidivism rate. The TRS Reentry Initiative will spend only $10,000 for 2 full years of support and reduce recidivism which in turn protects our communities and reduces the number of future victims of criminal acts. Based upon the evidence-based reports from similar faith-based organizations and their initiatives, plus the success stories from other TRS program participants, it is expected that the TRS Reentry Initiative will have a 90%+ success rate among graduates of the 2 year program.

❖ *Our Investment:*
Gold Canyon Heart & Home (GCHH) will provide the class materials, evidence-based curricula, support, and peer mentorship placements required to make this program a success.

❖ *Funding Request:*
We are requesting $1.4 million in funding. We are requesting these funds to implement this project for 100 participants for the entire two year cycles. This funding will include managerial and secretarial staff positions as well as the required funding for the one-on-one mentorship from certified peer mentors, financial education, Prisoner Assistant, Inc. bank accounts, active credit repair, credit restoration/creation, employability support, resume building, pre-release job interviews and placement, housing in a 2-3 bedroom home with utilities and rent paid for the first 90 days after release, health insurance, transportation, educational opportunities, pre-paid legal services, and continued mentoring which will take place throughout year two.

Creating and Managing
Multiple Income Streams

Learning to understand your true earning potential will open doors to many new opportunities for you throughout your life. A person's primary income is his or her job, but this is only a foundation for potential growth. If you take a second part-time job you have created a two income household. You manage these two income streams by making sure you are able to get to both jobs on time, take care of personal responsibilities, and making sure your health does not suffer due to lack of sleep or too much stress. Many reading this know all too well how working more than one job can cause "burn-out".

When creating a second income great care must be taken to balance personal needs with financial needs. One very effective way to manage this balance is to create or purchase a small business that fits comfortably with your current schedule and responsibilities. Many people choose a pre-packaged opportunity that can be built on a part-time basis. One such type of opportunity is a Network or Affiliate marketing franchise. These businesses are usually referred to as MLM (Multi-Level Marketing) in publications or advertising. Do not confuse MLM with the illegal ventures known as Pyramid Schemes. These fraudulent enterprises take money and offer nothing in return. MLM is about selling products and services and sharing in the profits generated. The network and affiliate marketing franchises usually offer support, training, and mentor coaching to help the participants achieve their goals. These opportunities have more flexible hours than many of the more conventional small business ventures or part-time jobs. Despite the extensive work involved, some people still prefer to actually open a small business from scratch using the methods described in the entrepreneurial lesson. There is nothing wrong with this; it is all about personal preference. Regardless of the vehicle you choose, the road is pretty much the same. When you enjoy what you are doing it doesn't really seem like work at all. This is the best stress management there is.

To learn more about MLM and other income streams, consult periodicals like Entrepreneur Magazine, Home Based Business Magazine, and other related titles. When it comes right down to it, anybody can create an extra stream of income. The key to success is realistic goals and good time management. Hard work and perseverance will give you the best opportunity for success.

Tip: The Direct Selling Association of the US and The International Direct selling Association are excellent places to start looking for legitimate network marketing companies and opportunities.

U.S. Small Business Administration

If there is such a thing as a "One Stop Center" for Business Ownership Resources, then the SBA (Small Business Administration) is the closest thing going. The SBA Loan is so common and so often sought after that most new and current business owners fail to utilize the many other services available from this valuable resource.

U.S. Small Business Administration   **www.sba.gov**

In Arizona:
Small Business Administration
Arizona District Office
2828 North Central Avenue / Suite 800
Phoenix, AZ 85004
(602) 745-7200 Phone / (602) 745-7210 Fax
E-Mail: Arizona@sba.gov / www.sba.gov

Note: Write or ask for a free copy of the "Small Business Resource" magazine. They will send you a free copy plus other useful materials within 7 to 10 working days. Here are just some of the services provided by the SBA:

- ❖ SBA Loans (Up To $3,000,000 Dollars)
- ❖ Tips on Buying Franchises
- ❖ Advice on Purchasing a Business
- ❖ SBA Micro Loans (Up To $35,000 Dollars)
- ❖ Grants For Small Businesses
- ❖ Surety Bond Program
- ❖ Small Business Advocacy
- ❖ Small Business Association Membership Information
- ❖ Business Start-Up Tips
- ❖ Training Network
- ❖ Disaster Recovery
- ❖ LLC and Corporation Advice and Information
- ❖ Business Plan Writing
- ❖ S.C.O.R.E. (Volunteer Counselors For Business Owners)
- ❖ Regulation and Licensing Advice and Information
- ❖ Tax Information (All Types)
- ❖ Certificate of Competency Program
- ❖ Small Business Vendor Database

(All 50 States have their own locations with the same variety of services)

Organizations and Associations for Entrepreneurs

The following organizations are excellent places to turn for assistance and answering questions related to opening and operating an entrepreneurial enterprise. These are groups of professionals with proven experience and success, and can be excellent resources for the entrepreneur.

SCORE
Counselors to Americas Small Businesses
800.634.0245
www.score.org

SCORE's extensive, national network of 10,500 retired and working volunteers are experienced entrepreneurs and corporate manager/executives. They provide free business counseling and advice as a public service to all types of business, in all stages of development.

With SCORE, learn how to write a business plan, apply for a loan, hone management skills and become a more confident small business owner.

AEEG
American Entrepreneurs for Economic Growth
1655 N. Fort Myer Drive, Suite 850, Arlington, VA 22209
703.524.3743
www.aeeg.org

AEEG focuses on legislation relating to capital formation, investment incentives and other issues affecting America's young growth companies. It works to inform its members about investment trends, entrepreneurial experiences and noteworthy events. The Venture Capital Alliance-AEEG is the only organization affiliate with the National Venture Capital Association, which represents the majority of the most active funds.

AEEG/s members are some of the most successful companies in the country. The organization develops relationships with local entrepreneur and venture capital groups in every region to support its members, networking and educations resources.

YEO
Young Entrepreneurs' Organization
1199 N. Fairfax Street, Suite 200, Alexandria, VA 22314
703.519.6700
info@yeo.org www.yea.org

YEO strives to help its members build upon their successes through an array of learning and networking opportunities. With more than 5,500 members in 120 chapters and 40 countries around the world, YEO/WEO (World Entrepreneurs' Organization) provides its members access to a dynamic network of peers on an international level.

The Young Entrepreneurs' Organization is a volunteer group of business professionals, all of whom are under 40 years of age and are the owners, founders, co-founders or controlling shareholders of a company with annual sales of $1 million or more. The YEO mission is to support, educate and encourage entrepreneurs to succeed in building companies and themselves. YEO offers global networking with access to top speakers, marketing materials, an extensive networking database, chapter development training, PR and media relations, support and workshops. There are many learning opportunities such as four-day seminars that combine keynote presentation, workshops, panel discussions and debates. Members may also receive published books to enhance their businesses.

NASE
National Association for the Self-Employed
P.O. Box 612067, DFW Airport, Dallas, TX 75201
800.232.6273
www.nase.org

The National Association for the Self-Employed is the nation's leading resource for the self-employed and micro-businesses. The aim of the association is to help the self-employed successfully meet the challenges of managing and growing their business by:
1. Securing focused tools and resources that help the self-employed manage and compete more effectively.
2. Representing the interests of the self-employed among legislators in Washington, D.C., on key issues that affect their business and that give these businesses more equal footing with larger corporations.
3. Providing access to benefits that promote the health and financial security of micro-business owners.
4. NASE also offers discounts on dependable products and services, assembles a group of financial services vendors that help meet financial challenges, and offers health benefits.

Edward Lowe Peerspectives
Edward Lowe Foundation
58220 Decatur Road, P.O. Box 8, Cassopolis, MI 49031
800.232.LOWE
info@lowe.org www.peerspectives.org

The Edward Lowe Foundation concentrates on "peer networking" by building relationships with other business owners who are dealing with similar issues in growing a business. The foundation provides information, insight and inspiration for second-stage business owners.

USASBE
United States Association for Small Business and Entrepreneurship
UW-Madison/Grainger Hall, 975 University Avenue #3260, Madison, WI 53706608.262.9982
jgillman@wisc.edu www.usasbe.org

USASBE is an eclectic group of government officials, directors of small business development centers and academics in fields like finance, marketing, management and economics united by their common interest in entrepreneurship and small business.

The organization is committed to empowering entrepreneurship from cutting-edge research to state-of-the-art applications and tools. It offers new initiative around entrepreneurship support organizations, opportunities for submitting grant proposals and knowledge databases such as Bibliography of Entrepreneur Research.

LESSON 14

**FINAL LESSON
INCLUDES REVIEW OF
ENTIRE CLASS**

GRADUATION

You review the Pre-Release section, and then go back through the entire course lesson by lesson until you have reviewed it all. Allow plenty of time for questions, and also add your own observations.

Pass out the suggestion sheets to the class and collect them. Be sure to read them because you will see whether or not the course was a success or not. You will also learn how to improve or change certain elements of your curriculum, and what needs to stay.

Pass out finished (typed/word processor) resumes and certificates.

THIS PROGRAM WORKS!

The inmates truly benefit from it and appreciate it. Don't forget to thank your aides, AND pat yourself on the back for . . . .

A JOB WELL DONE!!!

Student Graduate Questionnaire

Name (optional): _____

How was this class informative?

_____

_____

Was the way we presented the material interesting and fun? _____

If not, why?

_____

_____

What was the most important thing you learned in this class?

_____

_____

What improvement(s) would you make to this class?

_____

_____

Which topic(s) do you feel we should spend more time on, and why?

_____

_____

What was your favorite lesson, and why?

_____

_____

If you could add a lesson to this class, what would it be, and why?

_____

_____

Do you feel you improved your job seeking skills, and how?

_____

_____

Please add any personal comments or suggestions.

_____

Typing Services Provided By . . .

Paul Sparks. I am honored to have been a part of this momentous undertaking. I began this project as a contracted typing/editing job. While carefully reading the material, a clearer picture of Joe Chiappetta's mission began to develop. The overall concept of a book to aid those returning to society was sound, the product was sorely needed, and the timing was ripe. Editing page after page, I found increasingly more information that was pertinent and helpful. There were numerous "Eureka moments" where I discovered things relatable to my specific circumstances. Without having read this book, I would have missed or struggled with key elements necessary for a smooth transition to the streets.

After nearly three decades of incarceration, I am now pleased to be on the outside looking in. I have successfully bridged the transition back to society, and am pleased to report that I am supplementing my income through small entrepreneurial endeavors, hoping eventually to be able to work solely for myself. Many of the tools I utilized to realize these dreams were pulled directly out of **From Here to the Streets**. The information and skills provided in this book have proven invaluable, and I continue to employ many of the blueprints and suggestions found herein.

I am available for typing, editing, proofreading, and data entry for any project, large or small. I am dedicated to providing each customer a quality product while maintaining the highest degree of confidentiality and privacy. I have minimal overhead, and therefore am able to beat the rates of competitors. I am skilled, professional, knowledgeable, detail oriented, and deadline friendly. The satisfaction of the customer is my top priority; each client **will** be pleased.

Since you have read this book, I know you are open minded and willing to give second chances to help people pull themselves up and straighten out their lives. So . . .

The next time you have a project requiring professional typing or editing—a book report or a college paper, a project proposal or a business plan, a series of short stories or even the Great American Novel—why not give that work to someone who is trying to better himself and turn his life into a success story—someone who will go the extra mile to justify your faith in him?

<u>**sparkytyping@gmail.com**</u>
Or: P.O. Box 24-3664
Boynton Beach, FL 33424
Or Email to: joejr122@yahoo.com
Or Toll Free: 1-800-641-5964

Extra Bonus Materials

FEMA Free College Course Instructions

There are over 300 online classes to take, and the most important is the Professional-Development Series. This is a set of 7 individual courses that comprise the ***Professional Development Certification***. They are:

- ❖ IS-139 Exercise Design
- ❖ IS-230 Principles of Emergency Management
- ❖ IS-235 Emergency Planning
- ❖ IS-240 Leadership and Influence
- ❖ IS-241 Decision Making and Problem Solving
- ❖ IS-242 Effective Communication
- ❖ IS-244 Developing and Managing Volunteers

These independent study courses can be Googled individually or found on 22.fema.gov under the Emergency Management Institute—Independent Study Program pages.

All of these classes are free and open to all who wish to take them. They are PDF file e-books that can be downloaded and/or printed for use. The final exams are done online. There are several "usage codes" for what type of profession an applicant comes from to select, but "Other" will suffice. The exams are PASS/FAIL, and a 75% and up score is required for a passing grade. Upon submitting the final exam, the applicant will be notified via email whether or not they passed. If they do pass a PDF certificate is issued via email.

This set of 7 courses plus the separate certificate for Professional Development is a great addition to any resume, and also is useful for promotions or pay raises with any Human Resources Department. Each course has transferable college credits and CEU credit.

Each student upon completion of their first course is automatically enrolled in the Emergency Management Institute, and receives a transcript which shows the dates and the individual courses completed.

Ten Things Not To Say To Your Counselor or Case Manager

Counselors and/or Case Managers are probably the most misunderstood staff members in a prison. To begin with, they perform many tasks and have a wide variety of difficult responsibilities. They manage a case load. What is a case load? It's Release Packets, Levels of Supervision, Telephone Add/Delete and Trouble Shooting, Recreation, Orientation, Intake, Corrections Plans, Medical Care Directive Forms, Emergency Contact Information, and anything else that gets piled on. They also answer and forward Inmate Letters (kites); they teach classes, do legal calls, and may work on weekends at special events. On a daily basis, they normally cover hundreds of inmates on their case loads. Some of them cover twice that number. Because of this they are not always able to see us when we would like to see them. I recently interviewed six of them and asked them about their job. Based upon these interviews, the following are ten things not to say or do to your Counselor/Case Manager . . . if you expect to get positive results, that is.

1. "I need you to do this for me now!"
2. "Can I have a phone call?"
3. "How can I get out of this class?"
4. "You don't know what you're doing!"
5. "It's your job to do this!"
6. "You're never here to do your job!"
7. Poor manners in general. Respect is a two-way street. Spitting on the ground when you're talking . . . after you pull them up on the yard when they're walking somewhere.
8. Bringing frivolous issues to them. Common sense tells you what's really important. Frivolous issues don't need to be spelled out. They're obvious and easy to identify. Think about it first before you press your Case Manager for an appointment.
9. Using profanity when speaking to them.

That's how the Case Managers see things from their point of view. It's really just common sense. The system isn't perfect. Nothing always goes exactly the way we want it to go in life . . . in prison or out. The belief that, "I want it now because I'm entitled to it, and you have to give it to me right now because it's your job", is something that we would scold our children for saying. It's all about having patience and using proper social skills. When you want the best possible result you have to make the best possible attempt to get one. *Approach determines response", and "You never get a second chance to make a first impression."*

Expunging or Sealing Records

From AZLawHelp.org

Reentering one's community after the completion of a prison sentence is very challenging. Success can be difficult for many reasons. This article addresses one of the steps a person with a felony conviction might take towards overcoming barriers to successful community re-entry.

The outcome of any case depends on the unique facts in that case, the laws at the time of conviction, new laws that may apply, and the individual decision-making of the parties involved including the defendant, attorneys, victims, the Court, and any other interested persons.

Since the outcome of a case depends on many different things, this is for information only. It is not legal advice. An attorney can provide additional information and legal advice.

❖ *What is expungement?*

In Arizona, expungement means the same as "set aside".

❖ *What is "set aside"?*

Set aside means to cancel or revoke a judgment or order. Usually, the original record is modified or changed. The original is still available.

❖ *What is the difference between an expungement and a set aside?*

Generally, something expunged, no longer exists. It is gone. It is wiped out. On the other hand, usually something "set aside" is not destroyed but it is not the same as the original. In the case of a criminal record, the original may still be available for use.

❖ *Can expungement and set aside have the same meaning?*

Yes. The two terms can be very confusing. One reason for the confusion is that these terms are interchangeable sometimes. In other words, even though they are defined differently, they can also mean the same thing. Sometimes a record that is "set aside" is called an expunged record. Sometimes a record that is expunged is not wiped out and is actually set aside and can be used again. Note that in Arizona, expungement means the same thing as "set aside".

❖ *What does expungement and set aside have to do with criminal convictions?*

Expungement and set aside are tools that persons convicted of crimes might be able to use to lessen the negative impact of their criminal conviction and criminal record.

❖ *Does every state view expungement and "set aside" in the same way?*

No. Each individual state decides what expungement and/or set aside means in its state. States may look to one another to see how laws are defined, but each state makes its own decision about expungement and setting aside criminal convictions.

❖ *How does Arizona view expungement and "setting aside" convictions?*

In Arizona, expungement has the same meaning as setting aside. Expungement does not wipe out the conviction. The record of conviction is not destroyed. For the protection of the public, a conviction may be used to deny certain kinds of employment, licenses, permits, certificates as well as used against a person in future criminal cases, even though he conviction was set aside or expunged.

❖ *In Arizona, after a conviction is expunged or set aside, does a person have to disclose the expunged conviction on a job application or in a job interview?*

A person whose conviction has been set aside or expunged must disclose the conviction if the employment application asks whether the person has a prior conviction. An applicant must report previous conviction of an offense, if asked about prior convictions during a job interview. However, the applicant should also report that the conviction "has been vacated (or set aside) and the charges dismissed." The court uses this language in setting aside a conviction.

❖ *Where are Arizona's laws about expungement and setting aside a conviction?*

Arizona does not presently have an 'expungement' statute. The laws about setting aside a conviction are presently found in A.R.S. §§ 13-904 - 912. A.R.S. § 13-907 permits a person convicted of a felony to request a "set aside" of a felony conviction under certain circumstances. The statutes use the term "set aside the judgment." An application to have your conviction set aside may use the language "vacate judgment and dismiss charges." In this situation, "setting aside a conviction," means the same thing as "vacating judgment and dismissing the charges."

❖ *What does a criminal record show when a conviction is set aside or expunged?*

The law does not require that a conviction be removed from a person's criminal record. It is only required that the official record show that the conviction has been set aside. When a conviction is expunged or set aside in Arizona, a records check will most likely show the original charge and the original conviction. However, it should also clearly show that the judgment was vacated and that an order of dismissal has been entered in the case.

❖ *What are the benefits of having a felony conviction set aside?*

For someone convicted of a felony, a set aside can be very important because it has the effect of releasing the defendant from all penalties and disabilities resulting from the conviction with some exceptions. (See A.R.S. §§ 28-3304 - 3308).

Although there is a prior felony conviction, the record also indicates that the person successfully completed all court requirements and the Court vacated the judgment and dismissed the charges. This has the effect of putting the felony offense in a person's past as long as there are no present or future convictions. The focus moves to the present and to positive attributes, rather than on past transgressions.

❖ *What are the benefits of having a misdemeanor conviction set aside?*

For someone convicted of a misdemeanor, the benefits of a set aside are less because misdemeanor convictions do not impose the same restricts on constitutional rights that a felony does. In addition, a misdemeanor does not carry the same stigma in the community as a felony conviction. Further, there may not be the same barriers to employment and housing. However, some misdemeanor convictions, such as drug convictions, can present obstacles to employment and housing so a set aside may be helpful.

❖ *Who might be able to set aside a conviction in Arizona?*

A set aside may be available if a person was convicted of a felony in an Arizona Superior Court and that person has an absolute discharge from probation or prison.

If a person is convicted of a misdemeanor in a Justice or City Court and successfully completes all court orders, that person might be eligible to have the conviction set aside.

Note: A set aside is <u>not available</u> to a person convicted of a criminal offense:

1. Involving the infliction of serious physical injury,
2. Involving the use or exhibition of a deadly weapon or dangerous instrument,
3. For which the person is required or ordered by the court to register as a sex offender, A.R.S. § 13-3821,
4. For which there has been a finding of sexual motivation under A.R.S. § 13-118,
5. In which the victim is a minor under 15 years of age, or
6. In violation of A.R.S. § 28-3473, any local ordinance relating to stopping, standing or operation of a vehicle or title 28, chapter 3, except a violation of § 28-693 or any local ordinance relating to the same subject matter as A.R.S. § 28-693.

❖ *What happens if the Court grants a person's request to set aside a conviction?*

If the Court grants the application to set aside a conviction, the Court will set aside the judgment of guilt. The Court will dismiss the accusations or the information (the document that charges a person with a crime). Then the Court will order the person's release from all penalties and disabilities resulting from the conviction, except:

7. The penalties and disabilities imposed by the department of transportation under A.R.S. §§ 28-3304, 28-3307, 28-3308 or 28-3319, except that the conviction may be used if the conviction would be admissible had it not been set aside;
8. The set aside conviction may be pleaded and proved in any subsequent prosecution of that person for any offense; or
9. It may be used by the department of transportation to enforce A.R.S. §§ 28-3304, 28-3306, 28-3307, or 28-3319 as if it had not been set aside.

❖ *When might a person be eligible to get their civil rights restored after a felony conviction?*

A felony conviction results in the suspension of some civil rights which may include to the right to vote, hold public office, serve on a jury, and possess firearms. Usually, these civil rights are not suspended for misdemeanor convictions so this process may not apply. Again the laws change so look at current law and the laws in place when the person was convicted and consider speaking with an attorney. A person might be able to have civil rights restored if that person has an absolute discharge from probation or if it has been at least two years since that person's absolute discharge from prison. While the restoration of civil rights may be available to felony offenders convicted in a County Superior Court in

Arizona or in federal court, Arizona courts do not have the authority to set aside convictions or restore gun rights to persons convicted in federal court.

❖ *Will a person's gun rights be restored as part of restoring civil rights?*

Whether a person's gun rights are restored may depend upon the date of conviction, any court-ordered terms and that person's criminal and social history record. The laws may be different now from the laws in place when a person was convicted.

Requests to restore civil rights and restore gun rights are separate orders, but the request scan be submitted to the Court at the same time as the request to set aside the conviction.

❖ *How does a person apply to have a conviction set aside, civil rights restored and gun rights restored?*

To restore these rights, a person would file a request with the Superior Court in the county where the conviction occurred. For a federal conviction, a person would submit an application to the Superior Court of the county where that person lives. Instructions for all of these things can be found at the following websites:

- Coconino County: www.conconino.az.gov/lawlibrary.aspx?id=19434
- Maricopa County: www.clerkofcourt.maricopa.gov/faxondemand/300.pdf

If the county where the person lives does not have these forms online, contact the Clerk's Office in the county where the conviction occurred to see which forms could be used. Contact information for County Superior Court Clerks can be found at:

- www.clerkofcourt.maricopa.gov/CNTYCLKSLSMASTER2.pdf
- www.azsos.gov/business services/notary/AZClerks.htm

❖ *What happens after a person submits the application to set aside a conviction, to restore civil rights and to restore gun rights?*

The Court will review the application and may grant the request, deny the request, set a hearing or set orders the Court believes is appropriate in the person's case.

❖ *What can a person do if the Court denies the request?*

If the Court denies the request, a person can file a request for reconsideration, depending upon the reason for the denial. Instructs and forms for requesting reconsideration can be found on the Courts' websites.

(Sample Motion for Unresolved Warrants, Fines and Legal Issues)

NAME: _____

ADDRESS: _____

IN THE MUNICIPAL COURT OF THE CITY OF _____
IN AND FOR THE COUNTY OF _____

STATE OF _____	)	
	)	
PLAINTIFF,	)	CITATION NO. _____
	)	
V.	)	MOTION TO QUASH WARRANTS
	)	AND/OR FINE;
	)	OR, IN THE ALTERNATIVE SENTENCE IN
	)	ABSTENTIA TO CONCURRENT TERMS
_____	)	
	)	
DEFENDANT	)	
_____	)	

COMES NOW _____, Petitioner herein, and moves this Court to quash the warrants, complaints, or any citations that are lodged against Petitioner. The Petitioner cites the following in support of this motion:

1. That Petitioner has warrants, citation, and/or complaints under these cause numbers:
   _____

2. That Petitioner is currently incarcerated at : _____
   Serving a term of imprisonment of _____ year(s)
   His earliest release date is: _____ ;

3. That Petitioner is currently indigent and without means to pay fines herein, and that petitioner has enclosed documents verifying his/her positive institutional recode and programming.

4. That Petitioner would consent to sentencing in absentia to a term of imprisonment which would be run concurrently with the term he is now serving;

5. That the interests of justice would best be served by a dismissal or imposition of a concurrent sentence.

RESPECTFULLY SUBMITTED on this _____ day of _____ .

By: _____
                                                    (Petitioner)

STATE OF _____)
) SS.
COUNTY OF _____)

_____ , first being duly sworn, deposes and says:
That I am the Petitioner herein; that I am without means to pay any fines in this matter; that
I am enclosing documentation that the court may find useful in this matter; and that all the
information herein is true to the best of my knowledge and belief.

_____
                                                    (Petitioner)

SUBSCRIBED AND SWORN TO before me on this _____ day of _____ ,

by _____ .

_____
                                                    (Notary Public)

_____
                                                    (My Commission Expires)

WARNING!!!

This is only a sample of what others have used to resolve their issues. This is NOT a guarantee of legal representation or expected results. Everybody's case is different. If you can afford to do so, ALWAYS consult with an attorney first!